TEACHING THE BIBLE

A Practical Guide for Parents

CHRISTA ROWLAND

ISBN-13: 978-1721535897
ISBN-10: 1721535896

Author photo: Josh McCullock Photography
joshmccullock.com

Dedication

For the mothers and fathers who yearn to educate their children in the ways of the Lord. I pray for wisdom and confidence for you as you teach your children the Bible!

For my husband, Skip, who inspires me daily to follow God's call on my life. You are my best friend, a fantastic father, and an amazing role model to our seven children. Thank you for encouraging me to write this book.

And for Riley, Reid, Rex, Sawyer, Sutton, Sloane and Zeke...you are the best children in the world, and you are my greatest inspirations. To God be the glory!

TABLE OF CONTENTS

FOREWORD

Have you ever encountered a family that has an exceptional devotional life together in their home? Everything for them seems to be easy. Then there's the rest of us.

Family devotions, especially with children in the home, don't come easy for most of us. We plan and prepare for meaningful Bible study, but in the midst of life's pressures we tend to strike out. We long for that life where our kids desire to know God's Word. We want them to be eager to make a difference. But often, weeks turn into months and we realize that we haven't had that special time together. Then our dreams to build a spiritual foundation seem to slowly fade.

We wonder about our commitment. We make it personal. We ask ourselves what we are doing wrong. We get discouraged and let down, wishing for some remedy on how to make the Bible exciting for our children.

If you've ever felt like your children are lacking in their spiritual upbringing, this book has good news for you! It could be one of the most important books you've read in a long time. It gives timely advice on how to put daily devotions into a family routine.

Christa became my daughter-in-law in 2000 when she married my son, Skip. Over the years, Christa has made me a believer in her many talents and abilities. She is a loving mother of seven, and a dedicated homeschool educator. I've observed over the years how Christa and Skip have made the study of God's Word fun, exciting and entertaining, as well as an intensely deep learning experience for their children.

If *Teaching the Bible* had been written during my thirty years as a pastor, I would have presented a copy to each of my church couples as an example of challenging ways to learn God's Word with their children. If *Teaching the Bible* had been written during my years as a father with kids at home, I would have definitely shared it with my growing family. My wife, Judy, and I would have loved the opportunity to read this book early on in our parenting years. As a grandfather, it will be a joy to watch our fourteen grandchildren have the influence of this stimulating new book as they grow to love God, the Church, and the Christian lifestyle written about in God's Holy Word.

This book is both inspirational and bottom-shelf practical. May it challenge your heart to want to know God better.

Dr. Terry C. Rowland
Pastor, father and grandfather
District Superintendent
Oklahoma District
Church of the Nazarene

PROLOGUE

And these words which I command you today shall be in your heart. You shall teach them diligently to your children, and shall talk of them when you sit in your house, when you walk by the way, when you lie down, and when you rise up.
DEUTERONOMY 6:6-7

If you are a Christian parent, you are likely familiar with scripture passages like Deuteronomy 6:6-7, exhorting you to teach godly principles to your children every day. You probably understand the importance of exposing your children to a life of faith. In all likelihood you attend church regularly and pray together. Presumably you attempt to teach your kids the main tenets of Christianity as you guide them toward adulthood. But do you consistently read the Bible together as a family?

Teaching the Bible to your children might seem like a daunting task. After all, not many of us are pastors, ministers, theologians or Bible scholars by trade! Yet as Christian parents, we all have the responsibility to regularly and intentionally teach our children the Bible, the inerrant and infallible Word of God. But knowing what *should* be done and knowing *how* to do it are two entirely different concepts.

We had been parents for more than ten years before we earnestly considered teaching our children the Bible. We had lots of excuses. "Our children are young, and they won't understand scripture." "We take them to church on a consistent basis, so they must be learning what they need to learn about the Bible." "Well, they have lots of Bible storybooks, so they'll pick up the major Bible stories that way." And the biggest excuse of all: "Besides, we don't have time."

As a family, we had no meaningful, consistent devotional time, prayer time or scripture study time. Sure, we prayed together in the van every morning on the way to school and at mealtimes. Before bed, we'd read a Bible storybook...maybe. We at least prayed with the children every night before they drifted off to sleep. But purposefully teaching the Bible to our children was definitely not a priority in our household. Why?

Perhaps the honest truth was that my husband, Skip, and I were not diligent about studying the Bible on our own. We each had our favorite Bible chapters and verses that we'd read on occasion, and certain books we'd gravitate toward when we needed inspiration: Proverbs, Romans, the Gospels. We attended church faithfully, regularly participated in Wednesday night Bible church classes, and even led summer Bible studies in our home; but individually, we still struggled with daily scripture study.

And *time*! Our days were crammed full. Mornings were filled with school and work, afternoons and evenings were packed with music lessons, dance classes, soccer practice, dinnertime, and homework. By the time the tasks and appointments were all done, we were all ready to collapse into bed at the end of the day and the kids were lucky to get a bedtime story at all. Quick, hurried prayer time was all we could muster on many an evening before we caught a few hours of sleep and the whole routine started again the next morning.

But of all the activities for which we chose to make time, shouldn't Bible study with our children have been one of them?

Our lives dramatically changed in 2013 with the decision to homeschool our children. Up to that point, our young children had been attending the local public elementary school for several years. While we appreciated the hard work and dedication of their schoolteachers (several of whom we knew personally), Skip and I grew increasingly uncomfortable with the sheer amount of *time* public education was taking away from our family. When we learned that the school district was shifting from a half-day kindergarten program to a full-day schedule, our uneasiness grew. Our daughters were upper-elementary age, but our precocious and active son, Rex, was set to enter kindergarten for the upcoming school year. Try as I might, I could not imagine how my boisterous five-year-old son would benefit from being kept in a school building for thirty-five hours a week.

For many months, Skip and I diligently prayed about the future of our children's education, and we studied everything we could get our hands on about educating children at home. After almost a year of prayer and research, we made the decision to permanently withdraw our children from public school and start our homeschool with a fifth grader, a third grader, and a kindergartener, and our two preschool age children as well.

Suddenly, my husband and I were reevaluating all areas of our children's education. *We* became the primary instructors for all of our kids, who at that time ranged in age from one to ten years old. Up to that point, we had grown accustomed to other people teaching our children in almost every realm of their young lives; but in our new adventure of home education, our thinking started to change.

As we began to study curriculum options and research education methods, we came to the realization that not only had we been relying on others to teach our children reading, writing and arithmetic, but we had relied too heavily on others for our children's spiritual and biblical education as well. As longtime members of a wonderful church, we'd had no problem entrusting the Bible teaching to our beloved children's pastor and sweet Sunday school teachers. But just as surely as we knew God had called us to homeschool, we knew he was calling us to take the reins of our children's spiritual education and development as well.

Train up a child in the way he should go, and when he is old he will not depart from it. (Proverbs 22:6)

God gently yet persistently revealed to us in prayer and through scripture that *we as parents* were primarily responsible for the spiritual development and biblical education of our children. Our children, these precious, priceless blessings, were entrusted to *us*, and it was our God-given responsibility to be good stewards of our blessings. We began to fervently pray that God would equip us for the challenge.

So we committed to make Bible study one of our family's many subjects in homeschool, the first subject of our daily studies together. But where to begin?

Genesis 1:1, "In the beginning..."

That seemed like a logical place to start.

CHAPTER ONE

A PROBLEM OF BIBLICAL PROPORTIONS

Give ear, O my people, to my law; incline your ears to the words of my mouth. I will open my mouth in a parable; I will utter dark sayings of old, which we have heard and known, and our fathers have told us. We will not hide them from their children, telling to the generation to come the praises of the Lord, and His strength and His wonderful works that He has done.
PSALM 78:1-4

Twenty years ago, as a college freshman, I confidently slipped into my desk for the first day of Dr. Hal Cauthron's Introduction to Biblical Literacy class. Intro to Bib Lit was a required course for all students at Southern Nazarene

University, whether or not one was a religion major...and religion major, I was not.

I was, however, a fourth-generation Nazarene who had been raised in the church. Since I was a child, I had faithfully gone to Vacation Bible Schools, church camps, Sunday school, Sunday morning and evening worship services, and even Wednesday night fellowship. We had lots of Bibles and Bible storybooks around the house, and my parents took me to church whenever the doors were open.

So when Dr. Cauthron announced on the first day of class that we would be taking a Bible exam to test our general knowledge of scripture, I wasn't worried. Besides being a practically pedigreed Nazarene, I was also a straight-A student. Pencil in hand, I thought to myself, *"I've got this. This test is going to be a sweet, biblical breeze."*

Well, as Proverbs 16:18 says, *"Pride goes before destruction, a haughty spirit before a fall."*

To my shock and dismay, I failed the exam. When I saw my test score, my heart sank and my confidence shriveled. I had remembered some general facts, and correctly answered most of the questions about major biblical characters; but on questions about narrative, about Bible history, and about lesser-known figures in scripture? You might say my failure was a problem of biblical proportions. Most of my peers had miserably failed the Bible test as well.

Fortunately for me and for the other students, the grades for that initial exam were not held against us. The test was a potent and memorable exercise to show us all (even those of us who were raised in the church) that our basic Bible knowledge was insufficient and incomplete. There was obviously abundantly more for us to learn! We would all take the exam again at the end of the semester, after a course of in-depth study of scripture including narrative, context, and history...and to the best of my recollection, we all passed.

My class was not the exception to the rule; that same scenario of failure played out in every Biblical Literacy class at my small Christian college, with student after student, time after time, semester after semester, and year after year.

And if biblical illiteracy was a problem at my alma mater, located in central Oklahoma in the heart of the Bible Belt, you can imagine it's a problem everywhere. Over the years, the crisis of biblical illiteracy has actually gotten worse and worse in America.[1]

What is going wrong? How are young Christians, reared in the church and raised in the faith, reaching adulthood as functionally illiterate when it comes to the Bible?

Bibles, Bibles Everywhere

The *Guinness Book of World Records* acknowledges that the Bible is undoubtedly the best-selling book in the world. "Although it is impossible to obtain exact figures, there is little doubt that the Bible is the world's best-selling and most widely distributed book. A survey by the Bible Society concluded that around 2.5 billion

---

[1] https://www.barna.com/research/the-bible-in-america-6-year-trends/

copies were printed between 1815 and 1975, but more recent estimates put the number at more than five billion." [2]

And we know that especially in America, the problem is not one of access. According to the 2017 State of the Bible report from the American Bible Society, 87 percent of American households have at least one Bible; among Bible-owning households, the median number of Bibles owned is three. [3]

Even without a physical Bible in reach, technology has literally put the Bible in our pockets. With the advent of smartphones, scripture is more readily accessible than ever before. The YouVersion Bible App, a free app from Life.Church based in central Oklahoma, approached three hundred million downloads from around the world at the end of 2017.[4]

---

[2] www.guinnessworldrecords.com
[3] American Bible Society State of the Bible 2017, p. 26 – 27
[4] https://www.prnewswire.com/news-releases/youversion-bible-app-to-reach-300-million-downloads-by-end-of-2017-300568576.html

We own and have access to plenty of Bibles. The problem is, we own Bibles without *reading* them.

In a 2017 article for LifeWay Research, Bob Smietana writes, "Americans have a positive view of the Bible. And many say the Christian scriptures are filled with moral lessons for today. However, more than half of Americans have read little or none of the Bible. Less than a quarter of those who have ever read a Bible have a systematic plan for reading the Christian scriptures each day. And a third of Americans never pick it up on their own."[5]

Ignorance of both biblical history and ancient world history runs rampant in our culture. According to Jim Daly from Focus on the Family, at least twelve percent of American adults think Joan of Arc was Noah's wife, and a survey of graduating high school seniors showed that more than fifty

---

[5] Smietana, Bob *LifeWay Research: Americans Are Fond of the Bible, Don't Actually Read It* April 25, 2017
http://lifewayresearch.com/2017/04/25/lifeway-research-americans-are-fond-of-the-bible-dont-actually-read-it

percent of participants believed that Sodom and Gomorrah were husband and wife![6]

Sadly, many Christian adults simply do not read the Bible regularly in their own homes. We hear it read at church by our pastors and leaders, and trust that that is enough. We have convinced ourselves that church attendance alone will teach us everything we need to know about the gospel.

It is a blessing to have trustworthy pastors who are well-versed in scripture and teach Bible-based sermons. But hearing or reading the Bible exclusively at church is insufficient, and often leads to a superficial understanding of God's Word amongst laypeople. And a shallow grasp of scripture is particularly dangerous in our current culture, where the constant noise of news and social media exposes us to more and more *opinions* rather than *facts*. We don't need more people's opinions of what the Bible says. We need to know what the Bible actually says!

---

[6] https://jimdaly.focusonthefamily.com/joan-of-arc-noahs-wife/

My Own Bible Story

I consider myself abundantly blessed to have been raised in a Christian home by godly parents who deeply loved me and tried to the best of their abilities to successfully guide me to adulthood. I found Christ and was baptized at an early age, and my family attended church regularly, but I do not recall reading the Bible together all that often. It was more of a "special occasion" event. We read the story of Jesus' birth together before opening presents on Christmas, and we read the story of Christ's death and resurrection around Easter time. As children, my brothers and I were surrounded by lots of Bible storybooks, and as teenagers my mother gave us devotional books. But reading through the Bible as a family did not happen on a consistent basis.

I had my own New International Version Student Bible, which my grandmother had gifted to me on Christmas when I was thirteen years old. Inside the front cover, the inscription read, "*Dear Christa, I hope you will always love and use this book to light your way. Matthew 5:13 tells me that Christians are the salt of the earth and that you are the light of the world, like a city on a hill that cannot be hidden. Always let your light shine brightly for Jesus so that others may see him in your life...always remember that he loves you and I love you with all my heart!"* It was such a special gift; I felt honored to receive my first "grown-up" Bible, and I loved it dearly.

As a teenager, I attempted to read the Bible straight through on my own on more than one occasion. I'd start with confidence and determination in Genesis; although it's a long book, Genesis was full of interesting stories, so I would usually make it through. I'd still be going strong through Exodus – who doesn't love the stories of Moses, the plagues, Egyptians versus Israelites, and the miracle of the parting of the Red Sea? But then came Leviticus, and invariably I would get bogged down with all of the rules and the laws from thousands of years ago; they made no sense to my young teenage brain. And the genealogies and census reports of Numbers?

Forget it! I would give up and skip ahead to something more palatable, like the Book of Psalms or Proverbs, or I'd just go straight to the New Testament.

When I skipped around to familiar stories, I enjoyed reading the Bible, and I felt it was important to my Christian walk to at least attempt to do Bible study regularly. I found lots of scripture verses that inspired me, and a few that I committed to memory. Occasionally I'd use the index at the back of the Bible to look up verses for a certain topic, like "peace" or "grace." But honestly, when I reached adulthood, I had a limited understanding of scripture. Struggling to navigate the entire Bible on my own without adult guidance or input was intimidating. I never understood the Bible as a whole or developed a sense of the narrative of the Bible. I never contemplated scripture in the context of world history. I didn't grasp how the Old Testament worked together with the New Testament to point toward the gospel of Jesus Christ and tell the story of God's plan of salvation for humanity.

Does any of my experience sound familiar to you?

Do we not want better for our own children?

Perhaps Christian adults do not read the Bible often because such study was not modeled to them as children. Perhaps it is simply not part of the daily routine, because a consistent habit of daily scripture study was never formed. However, if you are a Christian parent, your Bible-reading habits (or lack thereof) are not just about you anymore. As parents we are models for our children, for good or for bad, as we shepherd them toward adulthood. If we ourselves are not dedicated students of God's Word as parents, it is no surprise that our children are not developing good Bible-reading habits of their own.

But is being well-versed and learned in Christian scripture *really* that important?

Questions and Reflections

1. What was Bible study like in your family of origin? Was it consistent, hit-or-miss, or nonexistent? How do you think your devotional habits in your past (or lack thereof) are affecting your present?

2. Reflect on your own biblical knowledge. Where do you need further study or shoring up?

3. Do you have a regular habit of reading the Bible with your children? If so, how could it be improved? If not, are you ready to begin? Pray and ask the Lord to help you as you start on this journey.

CHAPTER TWO

WHY IT MATTERS

Your word I have hidden in my heart,
that I might not sin against you.
PSALM 119:11

Why is reading the Bible important? If we are consistently involved in a solid, Bible-based church and hear God's Word preached every Sunday, does it matter whether or not we're taking extra time during our week to dive into scripture at home?

Yes! God reveals himself to us through scripture. Through the Bible, the Lord God communicates his character to us, teaches us his truth, leads us in the ways of righteousness, and shows us how to flee from evil and resist temptation. Diligent study of scripture allows us to know God intimately, so that we can lead fruitful lives that are pleasing to him. Thus, reading the Bible and developing a deep, abiding love for God's Word is not only important; it's imperative.

The Power of Scripture

Early on in our marriage, my husband and I were going through a time of significant trial. After a series of devastating losses, including a career, a home, and the loss of multiple pregnancies due to miscarriage, I hit an emotional rock-bottom.

Up to that point in my life, my Bible-reading habits were spotty at best. But during that dark time, I felt the Lord beckoning me toward scripture, and I consumed the Bible voraciously like never before. God used his Holy Word to speak to me, to comfort me, to constantly remind me of his love and mercy, and to assure me of his abiding presence in my life, especially during difficult times.

God also taught me to *pray* scripture when my own words failed me. During nights in which I couldn't even force my lips to form a prayer, God led me to pray through the Psalms; when I didn't have the words to pray, God the Father did.

"Hear my prayer, O Lord, and let my cry come to You. Do not hide Your face from me in the day of my trouble; incline your ear to me; in the day that I call, answer me speedily." (Psalm 102:1)

"Your word is a lamp to my feet and a light to my path. I have sworn and confirmed that I will keep Your righteous judgments. I am afflicted very much; revive me, O Lord, according to Your word." (Psalm 119:105-107)

"...I found trouble and sorrow. Then I called upon the name of the Lord: 'O Lord, I implore You, deliver my soul!' Gracious is the Lord, and righteous; yes, our God is merciful. The Lord preserves the simple; I was brought low, and He saved me." (Psalm 116:3-6)

I am ashamed to say that it took a series of crises for me to get serious about digging into the Bible. But God was good to guide me through that dark time with the wisdom of his Word. My husband, Skip, also began to study scripture in a new and more intentional way, and committed with a group of friends to read through the Bible in its entirety. Reading God's Word deepened our relationships with Christ, with each other, and with our Christian friends. During that painful season in our marriage, God used scripture to heal us, to encourage us, and to restore us both to spiritual health. Our marriage, our lives, our family and our circumstances eventually changed for the better.

My story is not unique. As Christians, we *know* that God speaks to us through scripture. What an honor and a privilege it is to communicate with the Lord in such an intimate way! If we neglect to read his Word, we are denying ourselves an avenue to hear from the Most High God. As parents, we are denying our children the same by not reading the Bible with them on a regular basis.

God Reveals Truth Through Scripture

In today's culture, it's sometimes difficult to discern what is right and true. Have you noticed that even our language has shifted? We no longer talk about the Truth with a capital "T" – instead, we hear phrases like "your truth" and "my truth." Well, what about *the* truth – God's truth? Through scripture, God reveals the truth about himself and about humanity.

When we read God's Word, he shows himself to us and we learn the truth about who God is. We deepen our understanding of his heart and his character. When we take the time to intentionally and deliberately study the scriptures, we gain a more comprehensive knowledge of God's mercy, his faithfulness, his grace, his patience, and overall, his sacrificial love for us.

I could fill an entire book with Bible passages about the nature of God, but I love this particular passage from the first letter of Paul to Timothy:

And the grace of our Lord was exceedingly abundant, with faith and love which are in Christ Jesus. This is a faithful saying and worthy of all acceptance, that Christ Jesus came into the world to save sinners, of whom I am chief. However, for this reason I obtained mercy, that in me first Jesus Christ might show all longsuffering, as a pattern to those who are going to believe on Him for everlasting life. Now to the King eternal, immortal, invisible, to God who alone is wise, be honor and glory forever and ever. Amen. (1 Timothy 1:14-17)

Amen!

Scripture study also reveals the truth about our sinful nature, and shows us how desperately we need the redeeming grace of God in our lives. The Bible teaches each one of us to acknowledge and confess sinful behavior, to repent and turn toward God, to ask his forgiveness, and to turn our lives over to Jesus Christ. But it's difficult to attempt to live a sinless and righteous life if we have neglected our study of God's Word and are ignorant of the nature and definition of sin.

How can a young man cleanse his way? By taking heed according to Your word. With my whole heart I have sought You; Oh, let me not wander from Your commandments! Your word I have hidden in my heart, that I might not sin against You. Blessed are You, O Lord! Teach me

Your statutes. With my lips I have declared all the judgments of Your mouth. I have rejoiced in the way of Your testimonies, as much as in all riches. I will meditate on Your precepts, and contemplate Your ways. I will delight myself in Your statutes; I will not forget Your word. (Psalm 119:9-16)

We rarely hear "sin" discussed anymore in any meaningful way. Even some churches neglect to preach truthfully about sin; we Christians sometimes have difficulty speaking truth in love to one another, and to nonbelievers. After all, we don't want to sound judgmental! Labeling certain behaviors as "sin" seems harsh, doesn't it? In an effort to not be offensive or "judge" anyone, we have lost the ability to discern right from wrong. But there is a difference between "judgment" and "discernment." And just as a muscle will atrophy without use, our discernment abilities are flagging.

As such, it's no wonder that Christians are having less and less influence over the culture at large. Not only are we unwilling to speak God's truth, but increasingly, we are ignorant of God's truth altogether.

Josiah Discovers the Book of the Law

The story of King Josiah and the people of Judah in 2 Kings 22 gives us a good picture of what happens when God's Word is forgotten. In the years before young Josiah became king at the age of eight, the people of Judah had forgotten all about their covenant with God. In fact, they had "lost" the Book of the Law in the temple! Bible scholars theorize that many years before, when King Solomon dedicated the temple, the Book of the Law had been deposited there – but subsequent kings had neglected to care for the Book, and it was forgotten. Ignorant of God's Law, the people of Judah were participating in egregiously sinful behavior including pagan worship, and they were neglecting to celebrate mandatory religious feasts.[7]

The story from 2 Kings tells us that in the eighteenth year of his reign, King Josiah ordered work to be done to repair the temple. During the

---

[7] Albert F. Harper, Gen. Ed., Commentary from *The Wesley Bible* (Nashville: Thomas Nelson Publishers), p. 557

course of the repairs, the Book of the Law was discovered, and a scribe named Shaphan brought it to King Josiah.

Then Shaphan the scribe showed the king, saying, "Hilkiah the priest has given me a book." And Shaphan read it before the king. Now it happened, when the king heard the words of the Book of the Law, that he tore his clothes. (2 Kings 22:10-11)

King Josiah was so devastated that his people in their ignorance had broken God's Law that he tore his clothes in mourning and despair! But having learned the truth, he led the people of Judah to reestablish their covenant with God and repent for their sins.

Like the people of Judah in King Josiah's time, our culture at large has forgotten God and the precepts and commandments he has given us. We cannot hope to lead people to Christ, change our world for the better, and influence our culture for the glory of God's Kingdom if we do not learn God's truth as revealed to us in his Word. But like King Josiah, we can rediscover scripture, repent of our sins and forgetfulness, and recommit to our covenant with God.

Scripture Teaches Us to Flee from Evil and Resist Temptation

We can learn about fleeing from evil and resisting temptation from Jesus himself. Matthew Chapter 4 tells us about the temptation of Jesus. Jesus had spent forty days and forty nights fasting and praying in the wilderness, and the devil came to him to try to tempt him and lead him astray. As Jesus was hungry, the devil first tried to persuade Jesus to turn stones into bread. How did Jesus answer? With scripture!

Specifically, Jesus quoted Deuteronomy 8:3, *"Man shall not live by bread alone, but by every word that proceeds from the mouth of God."* Those same words were spoken by Moses to remind the people of Israel about the manna that God sent from heaven to feed them in the desert.

So He humbled you, allowed you to hunger, and fed you with manna which you did not know nor did your fathers know, that He might make you know that man shall not live by bread alone; but man lives by every word that proceeds from the mouth of the Lord. (Deuteronomy 8:3)

The devil tried again. He took Jesus to the top of the temple and told him to throw himself off of it to prove he was really the Son of God. Interestingly, Satan also quoted scripture, from Psalm 91:11-12, *"He shall give his angels charge over you."* Ever the deceiver, Satan used scripture out of context in an attempt to manipulate the circumstances for his own mendacious purposes.

Jesus responded, once again, with the Word of God. In Matthew 4:7 Jesus said, *"It is written again, 'You shall not tempt the Lord your God,'"* a reference to Exodus 17:1-7, in which Moses admonished the people of Israel for complaining about the lack of water in the wilderness.

Satan tried to tempt Jesus a third time by showing him all of the kingdoms of the world, telling Jesus that he could have it all if only he would fall down and worship Satan. And Jesus answered him a third time, again with scripture. Jesus quoted from Deuteronomy 6, verses 13 and

16 when he told Satan, *"Away with you, Satan! For it is written, 'You shall worship the Lord your God, and him only you shall serve.'"* After that, the devil left him.

In this story straight out of scripture, Jesus Christ himself tells us how to resist temptation: by fighting sinful impulses with the Word of God. But a passing knowledge of scripture is not enough; we also see from this story that Satan knows enough scripture to attempt to use it to confuse us, and try to persuade and tempt us toward evil. We must be in God's Word daily to have a deep, thorough understanding of scripture so that, like Jesus, we can resist temptation, turn the devil away, and remain free from sin.

My Trial of Temptation

When my daughter Sutton was an infant, she never slept for more than a few hours a night. My husband and I tried everything in our power to help her, from changing her diet to getting her a CT scan. Every night she screamed incessantly before exhaustion finally caused her to fall into a restless sleep; a few hours later, she'd awaken us all with screams again. We had four older children to care for, and Skip and I lived in a constant state of emotional and physical fatigue.

I was certainly tempted toward despair and anger and worry, and I frequently felt like I was at the end of my rope, helpless and hopeless with my poor baby girl. In the midst of her screams, night after night with tears streaming down my face, I recited scripture:

"Rejoice in the Lord always. Again I will say, rejoice! Let your gentleness be known to all men. The Lord is at hand. Be anxious for nothing, but in everything by prayer and supplication, with thanksgiving, let your requests be made known to God; and the peace of God, which surpasses all understanding, will guard your hearts and minds through Christ Jesus." (Philippians 4:4-7)

I must have prayed that passage of scripture hundreds of times during Sutton's infancy. *"Rejoice in the Lord always..."* I was reminded to be grateful for the precious blessing that was my sweet Sutton, even in the midst of exhaustion. *"Let your gentleness be known..."* I was encouraged to be gentle, even in my discouragement. *"The Lord is at hand..."* The Lord was near to us during those endless nights - near to Sutton in her distress, and near to us in our fatigue and frustration. *"Be anxious for nothing..."* In a situation that was completely out of our control, God was in control. I turned my worries over to him. *"Let your requests be made known to God..."* I prayed constantly as I paced around the room with my inconsolable infant. And thankfully, God answered our prayers as she grew into toddlerhood, and whatever malady that had afflicted her eventually subsided.

You and I know from our own life experiences that evil and temptation have come our way. And it's only a matter of time before our children are exposed to evil and temptation as well. Fortunately, scripture has the answer.

But evil men and impostors will grow worse and worse, deceiving and being deceived. But you must continue in the things which you have learned *and been assured of, **knowing from whom you have learned them, and that from childhood you have known the Holy Scriptures**, which are able to make you wise for salvation through faith which is in Christ Jesus. All Scripture is given by inspiration of God, and is profitable for doctrine, for reproof, for correction, for instruction in righteousness, that the man of God may be complete, thoroughly equipped for every good work. (2 Timothy 3:13-17, emphasis mine)*

As Christians, we know that God speaks to us through his Word, revealing his truth to us about his nature and character. Through scripture, God tells us how to find salvation through Jesus Christ, and he helps us to flee from evil and resist temptation with the power of his Word. As Christian parents, we should do everything within our power to equip our children with the knowledge and wisdom the Bible provides. They, too, can learn from their Heavenly Father through the study of his Word; they just need you as their earthly parents to show them the way.

Questions and Reflections

1. Reflect on a time in your life when God showed you his power through scripture.

2. What truths has God revealed to you through his Word? Truth about himself? Truth about yourself? Truth about human nature?

3. Remember a time when God helped you flee from evil or resist temptation through knowledge of scripture. Or, think of a time when you failed to resist temptation because you didn't know the truth of God's Word, or had forgotten it. How could knowledge of scripture have inspired you to take a different course of action?

CHAPTER THREE

WHAT'S THE EXCUSE?

Therefore, you shall lay up these words of mine in your heart and in your soul, and bind them as a sign on your hand, and they shall be as frontlets between your eyes. You shall teach them to your children, speaking of them when you sit in your house, when you walk by the way, when you lie down, and when you rise up. And you shall write them on the doorposts of your house and on your gates, that your days and the days of your children may be multiplied in the land of which the Lord swore to your fathers to give them, like the days of the heavens above the earth.
DEUTERONOMY 11:18 – 21

Now that we have diagnosed the problem of biblical illiteracy and spent some time together examining why consistent scripture study is vitally important, we must acknowledge some common excuses for why parents are hesitant to teach their children the Bible. These excuses are painfully familiar to me, because for many years, the same excuses came out of my own mouth. The most common excuses are: parents have a lack of confidence in their own spiritual and theological education; the idea that children are too young to understand the Bible; the belief that taking children to church consistently is sufficient; and the most common excuse: the perceived shortage of time.

Excuse #1: I am not adequately educated in scripture and theology.

Even if you were born and raised in the church, you might not feel confident in your own knowledge of scripture. That was certainly the case for both me and my husband five years ago when we embarked on our journey to teach the Bible to our children. However, a lack of confidence or even a lack of spiritual education is not a valid excuse. As parents, our children are primarily *our* responsibility, and there is just no getting around that fact. We cannot abdicate our responsibility to teach our children the Word of God because of our own ignorance.

Ultimately, a deep understanding of scripture is necessary in order to present the full truth of the gospel of Jesus Christ to our children. As Christian parents, our primary goal should be to raise each child in the faith so that he will accept Jesus as his personal savior, and then go and make disciples (Matthew 28:19) to advance God's Kingdom on earth. The Bible is essential in guiding each person's journey to Jesus; we need to have a full grasp of the gospel in scripture in order to lead our children to Christ.

Educate Yourself in Scripture

If ignorance of the Bible is your primary roadblock to teaching scripture to your own children, then take immediate action to deepen your own knowledge and understanding of the Bible. Pray and ask God to create in you a heart that yearns for his Word, and ask him to help you establish a time for daily Bible study. If reading the Bible feels intimidating, find a good resource book that will help you navigate the biblical narrative, structure and layout. I recommend *30 Days to Understanding the Bible in 15 Minutes a Day!* by Max Anders. For creative ideas on how to approach Bible study, I recommend Rick Warren's *Bible Study Methods*. And be sure to have other believers come alongside you in your educational endeavors by participating in Bible studies and classes at your church.

If your church does not presently have a Bible class available to you, then start your own! Several years ago, I was in a season of life in which I was desperate for deep, Christian friendships. I was also in a spiritual dry spell, and I hungered and thirsted for the Holy Spirit to touch my life in fresh ways. I knew I needed to immerse myself in God's Word, but I wanted other women to join me on my journey. Although I was part of a great church, there was not an active women's Bible study at the time. I invited a few friends to join me and we started a weekly Bible study together. Every Monday night throughout the summer, we gathered in each other's homes to share coffee, dessert, fellowship and scripture.

Did I feel spiritually and theologically qualified to lead a Bible study? I most certainly did not; however, the Lord was faithful to equip and guide me as we went along. Our initial group expanded to include more friends, and God blessed that gathering of women beyond measure as we learned together, laughed together, cried together and prayed together. Our small women's Bible study became a summer tradition for five years in a row!

Around that time, my husband and I felt God's call to homeschool our children and start to diligently teach them the Bible. God used that small group Bible study to draw me closer to him, to deepen my understanding of scripture, and to give me the confidence and knowledge I needed to educate my children about the Bible.

If you feel your understanding of the Bible is insufficient, make sure *you* are studying scripture consistently, and ask God to increase your knowledge and wisdom. There are many things for which we pray that we are not guaranteed an affirmative answer, but thankfully, God promises to grant us wisdom if we ask:

If any of you lacks wisdom, let him ask of God, who gives to all liberally and without reproach, and it will be given to him. (James 1:5)

God Will Teach You as You Teach Them

As you teach your children the Bible, you will find that God is teaching *you* more and more as the days go by. One morning during our family Bible time, I read Genesis 14 to my children. The beginning of the chapter recounted a battle amongst multiple kings and kingdoms in the area where Abraham (then Abram) and his nephew, Lot, had settled. Amidst the fighting, the kings of Sodom and Gomorrah captured Lot and took him and his possessions with them when they fled. When Abram learned of Lot's capture, he took hundreds of armed servants and rescued Lot.

Then in verse 18, the character of Melchizedek appeared. I had read Genesis dozens of times, but I had never before noticed the verses about Melchizedek. Who was he?

Then Melchizedek king of Salem brought out bread and wine; he was the priest of God Most High. And he blessed him and said, "Blessed be Abram of God Most High, Possessor of heaven and earth; and blessed be God Most High, Who has delivered your enemies into your hand." And he gave him a tithe of all. (Genesis 14:18 – 20)

And then he was gone. That was it. Three verses out of the entire book of Genesis, and Melchizedek was not mentioned again.

I was intrigued! This character, Melchizedek, was an outsider; in later times, he would have been called a Gentile. He brought out food and wine as a show of kindness and hospitality, and offered a simple blessing. Abram responded by giving him a tenth of the spoils – the first tithe. It was a seemingly insignificant encounter, easy to skim over and miss, yet important enough to garner mention in Genesis. I had to know more!

I asked my children if they remembered the name Melchizedek from previous Bible lessons, and they did not. We dug in and researched what we could about this mysterious figure from Genesis 14. We read in our concordance that Melchizedek was mentioned two other times in the Bible: Psalm 110:4 and in Hebrews 7.

In Psalm 110:4, David writes, *"The Lord has sworn and will not relent; you are a priest forever according to the order of Melchizedek."* As we know, David was a king and not a priest. Yet as king, and therefore as the main representative of the rule of God for the people of Israel, he oversaw the work of the priests. Therefore, according to this verse, David was appointed to an even higher order of priesthood than the Levites and priests – a priest-king, like Melchizedek.

Hebrews Chapter 7 elaborates the story of Melchizedek even further. The author of Hebrews recounts the initial story from Genesis, then adds that Melchizedek means "king of righteousness" and King of Salem means "king of peace." Verses 4 through 10 describe Melchizedek as "great," so important that he collected a tithe from Abraham and was a priest even though he was not of the tribe of Levi, as later Jewish law required. The rest of Chapter 7 makes the argument that Jesus is like Melchizedek, a high priest *"in the order of Melchizedek, and not...called according to the order of Aaron"* (verse 11), but because Jesus lives forever, he *"has an unchangeable priesthood. Therefore, he is also able to save to the uttermost those who come to God through him, since he always lives to make intercession for them"* (verses 24-25).

I was blown away! The story of Melchizedek contained in those three little verses from Genesis was pointing to the eternal priesthood of Jesus Christ. Had I not been diligently studying God's Word with my children and regularly discussing scripture with them, I might have missed out on the whole story. Instead, God used our family Bible time to teach us *all* something fascinating and new.

At the conclusion of our biblical adventure that day, I expressed surprise to my children that we had learned so much together during our family time in God's Word. Rex, my nine-year-old, replied in a matter-of-fact fashion, "Mom, there's always something new to be learned from the Bible."

Excuse #2: My child is too young to understand the Bible.

A second excuse is that children are too young to understand the Bible, so you might as well just wait until they are older. It is true that there are parts of the Bible that even adults have difficulty comprehending, and it is not reasonable to expect a young child or even a teenager to understand every verse. I will suggest some creative ideas about how to teach the Bible to younger children later on in this book. However, do not let your child's age dissuade you from reading the Bible together.

Then little children were brought to Him that He might put His hands on them and pray, but the disciples rebuked them. But Jesus said, "Let the little children come to Me, and do not forbid them;

for of such is the kingdom of heaven." And He laid His hands on them and departed from there. (Matthew 19:13-15)

Through time spent in God's Word, we can follow the example in this passage and bring our children to the feet of Jesus. Let's not turn them away because they are young. You will be amazed at how much of the Bible your child can grasp with your help, especially if you find ways to teach the concepts in ways they can understand.

The Parable of the Tarantula

We were unloading our van after a week-long vacation when I heard Rex exclaim, "The tarantula cage is open!"

He had to be joking. "That's not funny," I said.

Rex's grandfather had assisted us while we were out of town by coming to our house and caring for our small pets. The night before we returned home, he had fed Timmy the Tarantula his cricket dinner and mistakenly left the lid to the terrarium wide open. Timmy was nowhere to be found.

My nine-year-old son was beside himself with grief and worry. I looked into his tear-filled eyes and gently said, "Rex, we're not going to panic. We're going to pray."

We held hands in the kitchen and prayed together. "Lord, your Word says to pray about everything. The Bible also says you created every creature, and we know you care about us. So we're asking you to please help us find Timmy. Help us to know right where to look. In Jesus' name, amen."

The children dispersed throughout the house to look for the tarantula. Outwardly, I projected calm confidence that we could fix this problem, but inwardly I wavered. I stood at the foot of the stairs and woefully surveyed the lower and upper levels of the house, mentally calculating the sheer number of places a Mexican Red Knee tarantula could hide. "We will never find this tarantula. Ever," I told my husband.

Undaunted, Skip gathered flashlights and headlamps and rallied the troops. In room after room, he had the children turn over tables, dump out laundry baskets, peer behind picture frames, and shake out shoes.

I decided we needed some more prayer power, so I texted the wives from our small group from church. They were all mothers, too, and I knew they'd empathize with Rex's distress.

"OK, girls, prayer request time. Skip's dad was taking care of our pets while we were gone and left the tarantula cage open. Rex is completely devastated and his birthday is tomorrow! I know it sounds like a comical situation but Rex is absolutely a wreck and it's so terribly sad. Thank you for praying."

My sweet friends immediately lifted us up in prayer. My teenage daughter texted her friends and asked them to pray, even though none are terribly fond of Timmy the Tarantula. And fifteen minutes later...

"Mom! Dad! I found him! I found Timmy!" Rex's cries of joy reverberated throughout the house. He'd found his tarantula underneath a side table right outside the master bedroom door. Rex scooped him into a bowl, plopped a plate on top, and delivered Timmy safely back to his terrarium.

Immediately, I texted my group of friends with the good news. "Wow, your prayers worked FAST! We found him! And what a great lesson to Rex that NOTHING is too small to pray about!"

That night during our family Bible time, we read the Parable of the Lost Coin.

Or what woman, having ten silver coins, if she loses one coin, does not light a lamp, sweep the house, and search carefully until she finds it? And when she has found it, she calls her friends and neighbors together, saying, "Rejoice with me, for I have found the piece which I lost!" Likewise, I say to you, there is joy in the presence of the angels of God over one sinner who repents. (Luke 15:8-10)

"Rex, what does this story remind you of?" I asked.

"Timmy! We looked everywhere for him!"

"Yes," I replied. "Just like the lady with the lost coin, you lost something incredibly important to you. We got the flashlights and lamps and looked everywhere, in all of the closets, under the furniture...were you ever going to give up?"

"No!" he said emphatically. "I wasn't going to quit looking until I found him!"

"Exactly. And that's how hard God is willing to look for us, for lost sinners. He won't give up until he finds us. And then he rejoices! Just like we rejoiced when we found Timmy, and we even told our friends the good news."

Rex's eyes lit up with revelation. His own experience that day with his beloved pet helped him comprehend the Word of God.

Look for Interesting New Stories

Once you start reading through the Bible with your children and venturing away from the more well-known stories, you might be surprised at which passages entertain your children. If you ask my children which Bible story is their favorite, you will not hear them respond with answers like "Noah's Ark," "David and Goliath" or "Daniel and the Lion's Den." No, their favorite story out of the entire Bible is the story of Elisha and the bears!

The first time we encountered the story, we were reading about Elisha's first miracles in 2 Kings 2. In verses 19 through 22, the men of the city were complaining to Elisha that the water was bad and the land was barren. So Elisha went to the water's source and poured salt into it, and declared that the water was healed and the land would no longer be barren. As I read the verses aloud, I thought that it would be interesting to discuss this miracle with the children after we had completed the chapter.

Then came verses 23 through 25:

Then he (Elisha) went up from there to Bethel; and as he was going up the road, some youths came from the city and mocked him, and said to him, "Go up, you baldhead! Go up, you baldhead!" So he turned around and looked at them, and pronounced a curse on them in the name of the Lord. And two female bears came out of the woods and mauled forty-two of the youths. Then he went from there to Mount Carmel, and from there he returned to Samaria. (2 Kings 2:23-25)

I finished the passage with a gulp, anxiously anticipating their questions. Would they ask why Elisha, a man of God, pronounced such a curse? Or why God sent bears to maul the youths? I closed the Bible and waited nervously.

After a few seconds of silence, my children looked at each other and burst out laughing! No questions about curses or vicious, heaven-sent, deadly bears, just raucous laughter at the thought that "Go up, you baldhead!" was actually in a verse in the Bible. For the rest of the day, I could hear calls throughout the house of "Go up, you baldhead! Go up, you baldhead!" And to this day, without fail, if I ask if any child has a special request for a Bible story to hear before bedtime, someone will holler gleefully, "Go up, you baldhead!"

Time in Scripture is Never Time Wasted

On the days when the passages are confusing or difficult, the children may not comprehend every nuance of every verse. Yet our "Bible time" is never wasted. Even if every word or concept is not soaking in, we are still creating the *habit* for the children by spending that time reading God's Word together. We are still completing the *practice* of intentionally studying scripture together. My children are growing up in a home where it is considered normal to sit around and read the Bible together as a family, morning and night, day in and day out...and that in itself is an incredible blessing!

I am also encouraged by the fact that we will revisit every bit of scripture over and over again as they grow toward adulthood. If they do not grasp every portion of the passage we share together, that's OK. I trust the Lord to speak to them in ways they can understand *in that moment,* and hope that their understanding of the Bible will continue to deepen as the years go by.

Ultimately, my goal with my children is to create a habit of Bible study that is so consistent and steady that they will carry it with them into adulthood. With God's help, I hope to raise lifelong learners who will seek out God's will for their lives through their study of scripture, even after they are out from under my tutelage. By reading the Bible together as a family, my husband and I are equipping our children with the tools they will need to one day make their faith and spiritual habits their very own.

When I read the Bible with my children, I take comfort in the words of Psalm 119:102 - 103, *"I have not departed from Your judgments, for You Yourself have taught me. How sweet are Your words to my taste, sweeter than honey to my mouth!"* Scripture is sweet! By continued exposure to it, my children will increasingly long for it. And although I helped orchestrate their initial exposure to God's Word, and though they receive encouragement from me to study it, God himself is their true teacher.

Excuse #3: Consistent Church Attendance is Sufficient

A third excuse is that if children are taken to a spiritually solid, Bible-teaching church on a regular basis, then extra Bible study at home is not necessary. I understand the temptation to think this way, because my family is fortunate enough to attend a wonderful church with an outstanding pastoral staff and a phenomenal children's pastor. While consistent church attendance is important, however, it doesn't invalidate the need for Bible study at home.

Our children's pastor, Marcus LeBaron, uses the following demonstration to illustrate the difference between time spent at church versus time spent outside of church. He stretches out a length of rope that is 168 inches in length – every inch represents an hour, and there are 168 hours in a week. In the middle of the rope is a piece of red tape about an inch wide, and that tape represents the one hour per week most children spend in church. One hour at church for every 167 hours spent outside of the church walls. Even if you take you take your child to Sunday school, church, and Wednesday night fellowship, that is still only three to four hours a week spent in a church building.

Even the best children's pastors and youth staff (and senior pastors, for that matter) cannot teach you or your child everything there is to know about the Bible in that amount of time. It's simply impossible. At best, what your child is learning at church should be a reinforcement of what your child is already learning at home.

Partnering Together

Work to incorporate what your child is learning at church with what they are learning at home. My children love to come home after church and show what crafts they made or pictures they colored while discussing what they have learned. If they have further questions about that day's Bible story, we make time to find more information for them in scripture.

If you're not sure what your children are learning at church, then work to get more involved. Volunteer in your child's class or elsewhere in your church's children's department to learn more about that element of your child's spiritual education.

Being a part of a church with a wonderful children's department is an enormous blessing. Take every opportunity to show gratitude to each teacher, staff member and pastor who has answered God's call to minister to children. But please understand that *you* as the parent are ultimately responsible for your child's biblical education. Rather than *outsource* your child's spiritual development to your church staff, you should *partner with them* for maximum benefit.

Excuse #4: We Don't Have Enough Time!

The final and most common excuse for why parents do not teach the Bible to their children at home is a perceived lack of time. In fact, according to the 2017 American Bible Society State of the Bible survey, the most significant frustration for adults when it comes to reading the Bible is that they don't have time to read it![8]

However, let's take a look at some of the ways the average person spends time. A large-

---

[8] American Bible Society – State of the Bible, 2017 p. 14

scale study in 2015 from Common Sense Media revealed that teenagers spend up to nine hours a day using media for their enjoyment, including listening to music, playing video games, watching TV, videos and movies, and using social media platforms. Tweens (children aged eight to twelve) averaged about six hours per day consuming media. [9] According to *Social Media Today*, "Astonishingly, the average person will spend nearly two hours (approximately 116 minutes) on social media every day, which translates to a total of five years and four months spent over a lifetime."[10]

Video games alone eat up an enormous amount of time in our culture. In 2014, Nielson 360° Gaming Report research indicated that Americans aged thirteen and over spent more than six hours a week on gaming platforms.[11] By some estimates, the average child will spend 10,000

---

[9] https://www.commonsensemedia.org/research/the-common-sense-census-media-use-by-tweens-and-teens
[10] https://www.socialmediatoday.com/marketing/how-much-time-do-people-spend-social-media-infographic
[11] http://www.nielson.com/us/en/insights/news/2014/multi-platform-gaming-for-the-win

hours playing video games by the age of twenty-one.[12]

In comparison, reading the entire Bible at a moderate pace only takes about sixty hours. As you can see, time is not truly an issue. We can make the time; we must simply take the time. Let's look for ways to discover time for Bible study in a typical day.

Along the Road

Deuteronomy 11:19 reads, *"Teach (these words) to your children, talking about them when you sit at home and when you walk along the road, when you lie down and when you get up."* Well, we don't do a lot of walking *along* the road nowadays, but we do a lot of driving *on* the road! With seven children participating in various activities around town, we spend quite a bit of time in our twelve-passenger van. Being in the car is a great time to discuss scripture; it's a wise use of your time, and you have a captive audience!

---

[12] http://www.chicagonow.com/between-us-parents/2013/02/kids-video-games-safe-benefits-length-time-play/

The other day while riding in the van, my five-year-old daughter, Sutton, decided it was a little too quiet, and was determined to start some interesting conversation. As Sutton has one volume (loud), she hollered the question, "Who knows what Jesus' first miracle was?" Before anyone else could answer, she gleefully yelled, "He turned WATER into WINE!"

"That's right, Sutton," I responded. "Who can tell me the whole story?" The children proceeded to recount the entire story from John 2. Jesus was at a wedding in Cana, and his mother Mary told him the wine had run out. He directed the servants to fill six large ceremonial washing jars with water, which he then turned into wine to be served at the wedding feast.

I turned to my fifteen-year-old daughter, Riley, who was sitting in the front passenger seat. "Who do you think would've been the first people to know about that miracle?" I asked.

Riley thought for a moment and answered, "The servants!"

"Yes," I agreed. "Think about that! Isn't it awesome that the first people who got to see Jesus' first miracle up close were the servants behind the scenes?" And that one little exchange morphed into a marvelous conversation about the importance of Christian servanthood and the value God sees in us serving one another in Christian love.

Opportunities like that are all around you! And it's not too late to start looking for them. Until your child is grown and out of your home, it is never too late to start a daily, consistent time of scripture study and prayer. It only takes a few minutes of time out of every day, but your child will know that God, his Word, and your family are top priorities in your home.

An old Chinese proverb reminds us, "The best time to plant a tree was twenty years ago. The second-best time is now." Don't waste time worrying that you should have started scripture study with your children years ago. No matter the age of your child, you can start today. By reading and discussing the Bible with your child, you are building the foundation for a lifetime of memories and a lifelong love of scripture.

A Matter of Stewardship

Another way to look at the prospect of diligently teaching the Bible to our children is to see it as a matter of stewardship. As Christians, we often think of "stewardship" as being a responsible manager of our physical belongings, such as our money or our possessions. Perhaps we consider good stewardship in terms of our time as well, and try to use our time wisely for the advancement of God's Kingdom. But, parents, I want to challenge you to take stewardship to the next level and realize that God is also calling you to be good stewards of the greatest blessings in your life: your children. And you must teach them the gospel of Jesus Christ, and prepare them to be good stewards of their time, talents and belongings as well – so you must equip them with the knowledge of God's Word.

The Sword of the Spirit

In his letter to the Ephesians, the apostle Paul writes that the Word of God is part of the "armor" with which Christians should equip themselves:

Therefore, take up the whole armor of God, that you may be able to withstand in the evil day, and having done all, to stand. Stand, therefore, having girded your waist with truth, having put on the breastplate of righteousness, and having shod your feet with the preparation of the gospel of peace; above all, taking the shield of faith with which you will be able to quench all the fiery darts of the wicked one. And take the helmet of salvation, and the sword of the Spirit, which is the Word of God. (Ephesians 6:13 – 17)

In reading about the "whole armor of God" and what each piece represents, did you notice the one weapon used for *offense* rather than *defense*? The Word of God! By teaching our children the Bible, we are equipping them with God's "sword," his weapon with which we can fight against the evil and temptation of this world; if we neglect our responsibility to teach our children scripture, we are leaving them defenseless. Parents, let's move beyond our excuses and start making time every day to get into God's Word with our children.

Questions and Reflections

1. Do you feel educated in scripture and theology? If not, think of ways in which you can remedy your situation.

2. What are your biggest excuses that have prevented you from studying the Bible with your children? What are some steps you can take this week to realign your priorities?

3. Reflect on ways you can *partner* with your church's children's staff, rather than *outsource* your children's spiritual development and education.

CHAPTER FOUR

LET'S GET STARTED!

*O God, You have taught me
from my youth; and to this day I
declare your wondrous works.*
PSALM 71:17

Bible study in every home will be as unique and special as each individual family. No two families will do scripture study the same way, nor should they! But I do have some practical tips and advice on how to get started. You will need some good Bible resources, a workable plan, some creativity, and a willingness to learn along with your child.

Choose the Resources

You will find a variety of resources useful in your endeavor to teach your children the Bible.

Here are some of our family favorites; a full list of recommendations can be found in Appendix A.

- *The New International Version Student Bible* – The NIV language is easy for my children to understand. This particular version also includes notes for further study, and "Bible Insight" sections to aid in comprehension of the scriptures.

- *The Wesley Bible in the New King James Version* – The NKJV language is more challenging than the NIV, but this version includes excellent in-depth commentary on every page. The Wesley Bible also includes a thorough concordance and subject index, a special section on archaeological discoveries, and nine maps with a detailed index.

- *Bible Dictionary* – A must for looking up subjects that your children may not understand, such as ancient customs, units of measurement or monetary terms. Bible dictionaries also include scholarly articles (similar to encyclopedia entries) to help you delve further into scripture subjects.

- ***Concordance*** – A concordance is an alphabetical index of proper names, significant topics and keywords that contains the main Bible passages in which those words can be found, so you can easily find all of the verses that pertain to a certain person or topic. Some Bible versions include a concordance.

- ***Bible Storybooks*** – For young children, it is helpful to have Bible storybooks on hand. I have found that my children obtain a deeper comprehension of the passages we read when they also hear the stories in children's books in language that is a bit simpler for them to understand. Our favorite storybook is the *Bedtime Bible Story Book* by Jesse Lyman Hurlbut. We use a tattered, well-loved copy from my childhood, but newer versions are available for purchase online. Hurlbut's book is excellent because it tells the story of the whole Bible, but it breaks it down into 365 digestible chunks. Every story includes the scripture reference, and you will notice that the stories appear in chronological order rather than in the standard order of the books of the Bible. The way Hurlbut arranged the book has been enormously helpful for my children in their understanding of the overarching narrative of the Bible. Additionally, each day's story includes thoughtful discussion questions. Another excellent storybook is *The Jesus Storybook Bible: Every Story Whispers His Name* by Sally Lloyd-Jones. This book tells the major stories of the Bible in a child-friendly, narrative form, and includes the Bible verse references for each story. The illustrations by Jago are beautiful, and will captivate your young children while you read together.

- **Bible Reference Books** - We use *The International Children's Bible Handbook: Answering Questions Children Ask – Genesis* *to Revelation* by Lawrence Richards. Although it was designed as a resource for the *International Children's Bible*, New Century Version, which is a Bible translation written for young children, you do not have to have an *International Children's Bible* to benefit from the handbook. The handbook includes added information about familiar Bible stories, gentle introductions to more complex Bible stories, excellent timelines, maps, illustrations, and a glossary. At the end of each chapter, real-life Bible application is encouraged with engaging "To Think About and Do" activities.

Select a Time

The next step in your plan to teach your children the Bible is to decide what time of day works best for family Bible study. Be creative and flexible; it may take a while to find the best time and get into a routine that works for your family. Since we homeschool in our family, we like to start our day with Bible reading as our first school subject. My husband is not always home for the morning Bible study, however, so we do evening scripture study time as well before the children go to bed.

We do not always get to do Bible study as a family twice a day, every single day – but that is our goal! We attempt to keep a consistent routine so the children know what to expect, but we are not rigid in our expectations, either. There are times when the morning is too hectic and the evening is too busy, so we will read the day's Bible passage over lunch together or in the afternoon. And it doesn't take as much time as you might think! Sometimes we have our "Bible time" completed in ten minutes; other times it may take thirty minutes, especially if the children have a lot of questions, or if we have gotten into meaningful conversation or have discovered a topic that warrants further research.

Don't get discouraged if you can't get your family together every single day to read the Bible, especially at first. Like any new habit or routine, it will take time to establish. If your children are older, you may find they initially resist the new routine, especially if it is something brand new to their schedule. However, if you are consistent, they will soon come to expect and even enjoy the new, special time together as a family.

Remember that the goal of this practice is not to create a new type of legalism or a new "rule" to govern Christian behavior in your family. The goal is simply to create the habit of regular scripture study with and for your children.

So try not to have an "all-or-nothing" mentality. If you can't come together to read the Bible every single day, honor God with what you *can* do. Can you read the Bible together Sunday afternoon after church? Can you read the Bible together on the weekends? Start there, and then pray that God will show you other times throughout the week when you can come together as a family over God's Word.

What About School Schedules?

In your family, do your children attend public school or private school, or do you homeschool? Each situation presents its own opportunities and challenges with regards to teaching your children the Bible. Let's look at some ideas for incorporating Bible teaching into each educational scenario.

If your children attend a private Christian school, they are likely already receiving some Bible training. For consistency, you could choose to align your family Bible lessons with the lessons your children are learning at school. Or if your children are learning about the New Testament at school, you might want to emphasize the Old Testament at home so that the children are receiving the full scope of the Bible's teachings.

In public school, your children will not likely have any adult-led Bible study time. But some schools have student-led groups; if you have older children or teenagers, encourage them to take their Bibles to school and study them, and pray with their peers when they can. Some of my daughter's teenage friends have started their own Bible study time at their public school during their lunch period. I fondly recall that the "Bring Your Bible to School" days were very popular during my formative years in public school!

With either private school or public school, you will have a challenge to make time for family Bible study. Besides the actual time spent away at school, your children will have homework and extracurricular activities eating into their evenings. If your evening schedules are too hectic, you might find it best to do ten to fifteen minutes of Bible study before everyone leaves for the day. Or perhaps everyone can gather together for Bible time around the dinner table, or before bedtime. Be flexible, and do what works best for your family.

If you homeschool, as we do in our house, you will have more freedom over your daily schedule in which to implement your Bible study time. We choose to treat scripture study as a "subject" in our daily class routine. However, our mornings get hectic too at times, with piano lessons, dance classes, and orchestra! On busy days, the temptation is definitely there to skip Bible altogether! But instead, we adjust. If we can't sit around the homeschool table for our Bible lesson, we will sometimes read our Bible during breakfast or at lunchtime. There have been some mornings where I'll have an older child read our scripture passage in the van on the way to a music lesson! We have had to learn to be flexible; but there has never been a day in which I regret squeezing in a Bible lesson.

I also attempt to add scripture verses into our other school subjects. For example, if the children are taking dictation to practice their punctuation and grammar skills, I will use a Bible verse. Sometimes they also practice their handwriting or cursive by copying a passage from scripture.

Whatever your child's schooling situation, you can find creative ways to incorporate scripture into your family time. Let's look at some ideas!

Make a Plan

Decide where you want to start in the Bible, and make a plan. Perhaps you want to start in the New Testament with the Gospels. Perhaps your church, like mine, has daily devotional readings for the congregation and you want to start with those. Some families like to read through the Book of Psalms or Proverbs, as those passages are fairly straightforward and easily understood.

When we first began our family Bible study, my goal was to read through the entire Bible with our children. So, we started at the beginning, literally, with Genesis 1:1. After a few months in the Old Testament, however, my husband and I both felt that we also wanted our children to regularly hear the words and teachings of Jesus – and we didn't want to wait out the months (or even years!) of reading through the Old Testament for us to get there. So, we changed our routine to include an Old Testament passage in the morning, and a New Testament passage in the evening.

In our home, I type up a plan for our Bible lessons as part of my weekly homeschool lesson plan. For each week, I look ahead to see what scripture passages we will read as a family, and then I check my other resources for additional information that might be helpful to the children. For example, we recently reread the story of Noah and the ark in the book of Genesis. We read a chapter of the story every day, and then I checked Lawrence's *International Children's Bible Handbook* for information on the measurements of the ark, Bible maps for that part of the world, and a picture of Mount Ararat. Then for the younger children I followed up at the end of the week with the storybook version read from Hurlbut's *Bedtime Bible Story Book*. Planning out the lessons takes a little extra work, but the resources and information add depth and richness to our family's Bible-reading experience, and that makes it worth the effort! I have included a week-long sample Bible plan in Appendix B.

There is another practical reason for planning ahead for your scripture sessions: if you have young children, there may be subject matter that you want to save for when they are a bit older! I am generally not a fan of "editing" the Bible, but I am also not prepared to have discussions with my five-year-old about terms like "harlot," "bestiality" or "temple prostitute" as we read through the Old Testament together! Planning ahead affords me the time to look and see what stories and subjects we can tackle as a family, and which ones we need to save for later when the children are older and more mature.

What About Uncomfortable Subject Matter?

The Bible is full of interesting (and sometimes uncomfortable) subject matter. Topics such as polygamy, child sacrifice, false gods and idols, rape and incest will come up in your Bible study if you read straight through – and that's just in the book of Genesis!

While your children are young, my advice to you is to pray about it, and then take each subject on a case-by-case basis. You may decide to skip small parts of some chapters and save them for a later time when your children are more mature; other awkward subjects you might deem worthy of immediate discussion after careful consideration.

Let's take the topic of polytheism as an example. As a parent, it is sometimes tempting to gloss over the subjects of false gods and polytheism in ancient history, even when mentioned explicitly in scripture. Perhaps there is a fear of confusing our children, or a sense that it's unimportant to discuss since we are in relationship with the One True God. However, I have chosen to address the subject repeatedly with my own children, as well as teach them about other world religions throughout history. Reading about false gods and idolatry is also a good reminder to guard against the temptation to allow the things of this world to become false gods in our own lives. I have found that the more we learn about idolatry, polytheism and other world religions, the more we can recognize the reality and uniqueness of our God Almighty. We truly serve a God like no other!

Another example is circumcision. The first time we read through the Bible as a family, my children were young, and thus we did not go into detail about the definition, meaning and purpose of circumcision in the Old Testament. I described it simply as a mark on the bodies of the Israelite men that set them apart from other ancient peoples. My children were satisfied with that answer at the time, and we moved on. Now, we are currently in our second journey through the Bible, and my children are several years older. My husband and I chose to explain the custom of circumcision in greater detail, as we both agreed our children were developmentally ready to understand it.

If you have a wide range of ages among your children, as we do, a solution is to have your older children and teenagers read along in their own Bibles as you read aloud to the family. That way, the older ones don't miss anything if you choose to omit some sensitive words or passages for your younger children during family Bible time. You know your children better than anyone else but God himself, so trust your judgment.

Surrounded by Scripture

In my house, I love to decorate with scripture. Bible verses are displayed throughout my home in various ways: via artwork on the walls, on papers taped to the refrigerator, and references written on chalkboards. I once joked to my friends that I have scripture everywhere in my house except in the bathrooms; then I remembered I have a painted sign in our master bathroom that says, *"I have found the one whom my soul loves,"* from Song of Solomon!

I have a few scripture signs that I have purchased, but it does not have to be an expensive endeavor to decorate your home with scripture. One of my favorite displays in my home is simply a verse that I typed up on the computer, printed out on cardstock, and placed in an inexpensive frame. The verse is Matthew 7:25, *"The rain came down, the streams rose, and the winds blew and beat against that house; yet it did not fall, because it had its foundation on the rock."*

God showed that verse to me during a difficult season in our early marriage as a reminder that storms will come – but if the "house" of our marriage is built firmly on the rock of Jesus Christ, our house will not fall. The verse is displayed prominently in our living room because I want my children to grow up knowing that stormy times are unavoidable, but with Jesus as their firm foundation they will not be overtaken by the storms of life. They will not just survive the storms; they will emerge victorious.

Another creative way to incorporate scripture into your family's day-to-day life is to have a Verse of the Day jar. At a recent meeting of our small group at church, our group leader sent each family home with a painted mason jar and sheets of Bible verses. Our pastors were preaching about God's healing powers at the time, and our leader, Allison, printed out forty verses about healing for us to put in the jars. The idea was that every day, a child would select a verse out of the jar to be read aloud and discussed as a family. We use mason jars in our house for lots of tasks, including drawing chore assignments and collecting quarters as a measure to discipline the children for various infractions – so my kids were delighted to see a jar meant for something fun!

I want to surround my children with the Word of God at every turn in our home as much as possible, in as many ways as possible. And by seeing those verses every day, we all easily commit them to memory.

Make Memorization Fun

We enjoy memorizing Bible verses as a family, and we make memorization interesting and fun by creating hand motions to aid in memorization, and occasionally setting the verses to music. Children have an amazing capacity for memorization, so work to hide God's Word in their hearts while you can! Since many of my children are still young, we are not overly ambitious; we usually focus on one verse or passage a month. Typically, we pair a memorization verse with a particular character quality we are aiming to develop in our children.

Memorization of scripture is an important component of Bible study. In her book *How to Read the Bible So It Changes Your Life,* author Aletha Hinthorn writes, "The best way to make a verse come alive in our spirits is to memorize it. As we go through the day reflecting on it, the Holy Spirit helps us understand what it means. 'Reflect on what I am saying, for the Lord will give you insight into all of this' (2 Tim. 2:7). When we've tucked His words into the inner recesses of our hearts, God's Word comes to mind just at the moment when we need a promise or a command. We then gain understanding – practical knowledge of how to put the insight into practice."[13]

Music is a wonderful way to help children memorize scripture. We all remember songs from our childhood, don't we? I can still remember songs like "Zacchaeus Was a Wee Little Man" and "Father Abraham!" Nowadays, you can find CDs to

---

[13] Aletha Hinthorn, *How to Read the Bible So It Changes Your Life* (Kansas City: Beacon Hill Press, 2004), 44.

aid in scripture memorization on Amazon, Bible verse song videos on YouTube, and fun scripture songs on iTunes. The possibilities are endless!

Keep Them Engaged

My children certainly have their favorite books of the Bible, and stories that they ask to hear repeatedly. There are other parts that do not excite them or interest them as much – but instead of skipping those lesser-loved passages, we read through them together.

To keep them engaged on those days, I will have them join in to say parts of the passage aloud with me. For example, we recently started re-reading the book of Genesis. In the latter half of Chapter 11, there is a genealogy of the descendants of Shem, tracing the lineage from Shem down to Terah, who was Abraham's father. Admittedly, Bible genealogies can be pretty dry, but I noticed that every verse ended with the same series of words.

Two years after the flood, when Shem was 100 years old, he became the father of Arphaxad.

*And after he became the father of Arphaxad, Shem lived 500 years **and had other sons and daughters.*** *(Genesis 11:10-11, emphasis mine)*

For the rest of the chapter, every time I came across the words "and had other sons and daughters," I pointed to the children and they chanted the words aloud with me. It was a simple yet effective way to engage the kids and make sure they were paying attention at the same time.

Get Creative!

I wish I could tell you that during Bible time, my children sit perfectly still and quiet with their hands folded, enraptured with the sound of my voice and hanging on my every word. That, however, is far from our reality!

My children are active listeners, meaning they are much more attentive if they are *doing* something constructive while listening. I keep lots of paper, markers and crayons on hand, and they are always permitted to draw pictures while I am reading. My only rule is that whatever they are drawing must pertain to the passage we are studying. Even my oldest children enjoy it! My daughter, Reid, has gotten into the habit of drawing elaborate comic strip–style cartoons for each Bible story. Her depiction of Absalom, complete with beautiful, flowing cartoon hair is truly something to behold! Sometimes the children sculpt with play dough or build structures with blocks or Legos. As long as they play quietly, and as long as their handiwork has something to do with the story, they are free to make it fun. When we are done reading through our Bible passage, the children always enjoy telling me about their drawings and creations.

Abimelech

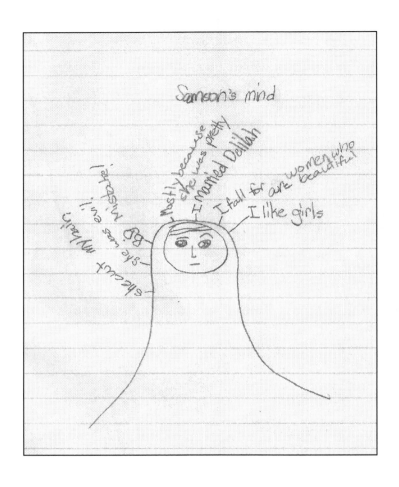

Here are some of Reid's illustrations!

We do our best to have fun and get creative! I have sat through many a dramatic interpretation of scripture. My children have enlisted their long-suffering father to play a variety of characters from Goliath (as he is the tallest person in the house) to the donkey that carried Mary to Bethlehem (as he is also the most amenable person in the house, and willing to wear long socks on his ears). Fortunately, I am usually just cast as the narrator! We have told Bible stories with paper bag puppets, and acted out scripture passages using stuffed animals. My husband and I do what we can to help focus the children's attention while making the experience enjoyable and memorable for the whole family.

When you are reading the Bible with your children, think of creative ways to engage them. Young children, especially, learn from *seeing* and *doing*, not just *listening*. Embrace their active learning styles and walk outside to mark out the measurements of Noah's ark. Build a tent and talk about Abraham. Make mud bricks while reading about the Israelites in Egypt. Look for locusts and frogs while reading about the plagues. Plant some seeds while reading the Parable of the Sower. The Bible is full of language about the magnificence and beauty of God's creation, so go out and experience it!

Bring the Bible to Life

Another tip is to "bring the Bible to life" at every opportunity you have. What activities can you participate in as a family that will inspire a deeper understanding of God's Word?

Although we are Christian and not Jewish, we have a tradition of holding a Passover Seder with family friends every year around Easter time. Our dear friends, Jon and Blaire, along with their children, welcome us into their home to hold the "feast." Blaire prepares a Seder plate for each guest with symbolic Passover food including parsley, horseradish (the "bitter herb"), charoset (a mixture of honey, fruits and nuts), roasted lamb (representing the shank bone), and a boiled egg. A basket of matzah bread is placed on the table, along with several cups for grape juice.

The adults then take turns reading passages from the Old Testament about the Exodus from Egypt, and we read a script reminding us what each special food symbolizes. The matzah reminds us that the Israelites did not have time to bake leavened bread for their journey out of Egypt once Pharaoh allowed them to leave, so they quickly made unleavened dough. The parsley represents the experience of the Israelites initially thriving in Egypt; then everyone dips the parsley into salt water before taking a bite to remember the tears shed by the Israelites once the pharaoh enslaved them. The horseradish represents the bitterness of slavery; the charoset represents the mortar the Israelites used when laying bricks ordered by the pharaoh. The lamb meat represents the sacrifice the Israelites offered to God the night before their exodus. And the egg represents a festival sacrifice that the Israelites once offered in the Temple of Jerusalem.[14]

The children usually conclude the Passover Seder with some sort of dramatic performance about the Exodus. It is always an amazing educational experience as well as a spiritual one; and now, when the Passover feast is referenced throughout the Bible, my children have a good

---

[14] https://www.everydayhealth.com/diet-nutrition/7-symbolic-foods-passover

idea of what that meant to the Israelites, because they have experienced a version of it themselves.

Our children look forward to learning about the rituals, hearing the scripture passages, listening to the Exodus story, and eating the special Passover foods every single year. In fact, every other time we go to Jon and Blaire's house to visit throughout the year, my son Sawyer asks, "Are we going to eat parsley and boiled eggs?"

Scripture in Daily Activities

I also love to look for opportunities to discuss scripture with my children in day-to-day life. Last February, when the Oklahoma weather was especially gray and wintery, I attempted to bring a little "spring" into the house. My five-year-old daughter, Sutton, and I started some seeds indoors.

We prepared little biodegradable seedling cups with potting soil, and chose a variety of seeds to sow together in anticipation of planting the seedlings outside when the weather warmed up. After planting the seeds, I meticulously labeled each set of seedling cups with a permanent marker, and Sutton and I took turns carefully watering each tiny container of soil.

Several days later, much to Sutton's excitement, tiny green shoots had begun to sprout up out of the dirt. But to my dismay, the permanent marker had become completely illegible, the ink running and blurry from the water seeping through the biodegradable material of the seed containers.

"Oh no," I sighed. "Now I can't tell which plant is which!"

Sutton nonchalantly declared, "It's OK, Mom. The plants will tell us what they are growing when they get bigger."

And just like that, with a simple conversation about plants, I had an opportunity to discuss scripture with my child. Plants grow what they grow, and we would know soon enough what type of food each plant would bear. Jesus used similar language in Luke 6 when he said,

"For a good tree does not bear bad fruit, nor does a bad tree bear good fruit. For every tree is

known by its own fruit. For men do not gather figs from thorns, nor do they gather grapes from a bramble bush. A good man out of the good treasure of his heart brings forth good; and an evil man out of the evil treasure of his heart brings forth evil. For out of the abundance of the heart his mouth speaks." (Luke 6:43 – 45)

Look for every opportunity to bring the Bible into your day-to-day conversations with your children. Ask God to help you recognize such opportunities. Not every conversation needs to be a Bible lesson, but opportunities abound for fruitful discussion inspired by God's Word.

God Equips When He Calls

Parents, your Heavenly Father is faithful to help you in your endeavors to teach your children. God is good to take our everyday experiences and use them as opportunities to turn to scripture. I like to think of such opportunities as "windows" into his Word. Don't be intimidated by the thought of teaching scripture to your children. With good resources, a little planning, and some creativity, you and your children can enjoy learning about the Bible together. As a Christian parent, God has called *you* to take charge of your children's spiritual development and education, and the good news is that God is always faithful to equip when he calls.

Questions and Reflections

1. Reflect on your typical weekly family schedule. When would be a good time for family Bible study? Would mornings work best? Dinnertime or bedtime? If you can't do every day right now, on what days *can* you schedule some Bible time? Pray and ask God to show you what is best for your family.

2. Make a list of supplies and resources that will be helpful as you embark on your journey through the Bible with your children.

3. What are some creative ways you can "surround yourself" with scripture in your home?

4. What action steps are you ready to take to begin family Bible study in your own household?

CHAPTER FIVE

BEYOND BIBLE STORIES

For the Word of God is living and powerful, and sharper than any two-edged sword, piercing even to the division of soul and spirit, and of joints and marrow, and is a discerner of the thoughts and intents of the heart.

HEBREWS 4:12

Once you have established a Bible-reading plan and routine with your children, look for ways to deepen your family's understanding of God's Word. In our home, we intentionally work to increase our knowledge by reading the Bible in its entirety, rather than as separate Bible stories; by learning about ancient history and geography; and by studying the context of Bible times.

Read the Entire Bible

Most of us who grew up in a Christian home have memories of learning Bible stories. Bible stories and storybooks are wonderful tools to help spark initial interest in the Bible; often children gravitate toward their favorite stories over and over again. With young children, there is a temptation to just use the Bible storybooks or pick and choose the favorite scripture stories. However, I believe you should use the whole Word of God as your primary source for teaching stories from the Bible, and consider using the storybooks as supplements.

The Bible tells us everything we need to know for our personal salvation and spiritual health. It teaches about God's deep and abiding love for us, about the truth of our sinful nature, about Jesus' offer of salvation through his death on the cross, and how to live righteously in a way that is holy and pleasing to God. But going beyond Bible stories and reading the Bible in its entirety helps teach our children that the Bible is also a *narrative*. By that, I mean that the Bible is more than a collection of separate events in verses, chapters, and different books; rather, it is a *narrative* of the history of the nation of Israel and the greater story of God's redemption of humanity through the death and resurrection of his son, Jesus Christ.

Writing for The Gospel Coalition website, author Trevin Wax gives four reasons to teach the Bible's storyline – what I have referred to as the "narrative" of scripture. His first reason is to gain a biblical worldview and to avoid being a Christian who does not have a Christian worldview. Second, he writes that it is important to learn the Bible's storyline in order to have the ability to recognize false worldviews and reject them. His third reason to know the Bible narrative is to have an accurate understanding of the gospel, as the story of the Bible gives the full context to the message about Jesus Christ. And fourth, studying the biblical storyline will keep our focus on Christ.[15]

---

[15] https://www.thegospelcoalition.org/blogs/trevin-wax/4-reasons-to-teach-the-bibles-storyline/

Wax writes, "Here's what happens if we learn individual Bible stories and never connect them to the big Story. We put ourselves in the scene as if we are the main character. We take the moral examples of the Old and New Testament as if they were there to help us along in the life we've chosen for ourselves.

"But the more we read the Bible, the more we see that God is the main character, not us...We're the ones who need rescue, who need a Savior who will deliver us from Satan, sin and death."[16]

A final reason to teach the Bible in its entirety is to show the *complete* picture of each Bible story to our children. Bible storybooks (and even some Bible curricula) written for children tend to present Bible characters as heroes, seemingly greater than mortal men. While characters such as Abraham, Moses, and David, to name a few, certainly accomplished heroic feats with the help of God, they were not *perfect* men.

---

[16] https://www.thegospelcoalition.org/blogs/trevin-wax/4-reasons-to-teach-the-bibles-storyline/

When teaching the stories of these Bible heroes to our children, it is extremely important to present the entire story from the Bible. We should do this because our children must know in the depths of their souls that just as God used painfully imperfect, chronically *human* people to advance his kingdom in Bible times, he can use *us* as well – flaws, imperfections, sinful natures and all – if we will turn to him, repent of our sins, and follow his will.

Help Your Child Understand History

Most likely, many of us initially learned about the Bible at church or in the home, and not at school. Consequently, there is a temptation to view Bible history in a vacuum, as if Bible events did not occur in the same timeline as ancient world history. In our home, we study Bible history and ancient world history together to give the children a clear picture of when biblical events actually took place in the scope of human history.

Studying scripture within the framework of ancient world history has several benefits. As learners we get a more accurate picture of what life was truly like for God's people during Bible times. Studying Bible history and world history together also gives us a deeper understanding about the ways in which the world changed over the more than two thousand years spanning from the beginning of the Old Testament to the end of the New Testament. In addition, we get a keen sense of the unique ways in which God intervened in history to redeem his people.

Abraham in History

Let's use the story of Abraham from the book of Genesis as our first example of how an understanding of world history leads to a deeper comprehension of the Bible. We know from Genesis 11 that Abraham's family, led by his father, Terah, set out from Ur to head for Canaan, but eventually settled in Haran. It was there that Abraham (then Abram), at the age of seventy-five, heard the call from the Lord to leave his country and go to the land of Canaan. The Lord also promised,

"I will make you a great nation; I will bless you and make your name great; and you shall be a blessing. I will bless those who bless you, and I will curse him who curses you; and in you all the families of the earth shall be blessed." (Genesis 12:2-3)

Most of us who were raised in the church are familiar with this story. But to more deeply understand the magnitude of the significance of this encounter with God, let's take a quick look at what was going on in the lands surrounding Abraham when he received the call from the Lord.

Abraham came from the land of Ur of the Chaldeans beside the Euphrates River in Mesopotamia, during a time that is referred to in history as the Middle Bronze Age. It was a time of pervasive polytheism. The moon god, Nanna, was the chief deity worshiped in both Ur and Haran, although there was a vast array of deities worshiped in that part of the world during that time. Scripture tells us that even Abraham's father, Terah, worshiped other gods:

And Joshua said to all the people, "Thus says the Lord God of Israel: 'Your fathers, including

Terah, the father of Abraham and the father of Nahor, dwelt on the other side of the River in old times; and they served other gods.'" (Joshua 24:2)

What else was going on in the world during Abraham's time? While scholars disagree on the exact dates of his lifetime, we know that he lived sometime around 2000 BC, and moved with his people to Canaan around 1800 BC. Elsewhere in the world at that time, civilizations were bustling and busy. From 1900 BC to 1450 BC, the Minoans were building palaces on Crete. The Middle Kingdom of Egypt began in 2040 BC; the Hittites settled in Anatolia in 2000 BC; the people of the Indus Valley in South Asia were at the peak of their success around that time as well.[17]

Before Abraham's lifetime, major events from the Bible include Creation, the story of Adam and Eve in the Garden of Eden, and Noah and the Great Flood. But major events in ancient world history had occurred as well. Consider that by the time Abraham walked the earth, initial building

---

[17] Jane Bingham, Fiona Chandler and Sam Taplin, *The Usborne Encyclopedia of World History* (London: Usborne Publishing, Ltd., 2000), p. 394 - 395

phases of Stonehenge had already been completed (starting in 3000 BC) and the Egyptians had started building the Great Pyramid at Giza (2530 BC)![18]

When one knows a little more about the events of the world and the culture surrounding Abram and his family, the significance of the One True God revealing himself to Abram becomes acutely apparent. Out of all of human history and all of the civilizations around the ancient world, God chose Abram. The Lord spoke directly to him, beckoning him out of the polytheism of Abram's own family and surrounding culture and into a direct relationship with God himself. Thus, Abram was the first known monotheist.[19]

Before studying ancient history alongside the Bible, I marveled at Abram's faith in God and his willingness to leave everything he knew in hopes of receiving a yet-unseen promise from the

[18] Jane Bingham, Fiona Chandler and Sam Taplin, *The Usborne Encyclopedia of World History* (London: Usborne Publishing, Ltd., 2000), p. 394

[19] Susan Wise Bauer, *The History of the Ancient World: From the Earliest Accounts to the Fall of Rome* (New York: W.W. Norton & Company, Inc.; 2007), p. 127

Lord. Now, as I contemplate the Bible within the framework of ancient human history, I am astounded and astonished by the loving character of God the Redeemer. The One True God, who desired restoration with his created people after the Fall, revealed himself to Abram, called him out of obscurity, changed his name to Abraham, and made him part of God's plan to reconcile humanity unto himself.

Rome Hits Home

In our family, our children love to learn about ancient world history, and one of their favorite civilizations to study is the Roman Empire. They are intrigued by all aspects of ancient Roman culture. And as we studied the Bible alongside ancient history, it didn't take the children long to make the connection that the Romans mentioned in the Bible were the same Romans with whom they were fascinated in their history books. For deeper understanding, we read the story of Jesus within the full context and history of the surrounding culture of the Roman Empire.

In the Gospels, there are numerous mentions of Rome and officials of the Roman Empire. A census ordered by Roman leaders brought Mary and Joseph to Bethlehem, where Jesus was born:

And it came to pass in those days that a decree went out from Caesar Augustus that all the world should be registered. This census first took place while Quirinius was governing Syria. So all went to be registered, everyone to his own city. (Luke 2:1-3)

Caesar Augustus was the Roman emperor at the time, and Quirinius was a high-ranking Roman official. There are other references to Rome and Roman officials throughout the books of Matthew, Mark, Luke and John, the most famous account being the story of Jesus' trial before Pontius Pilate, the Roman governor.

Later in the New Testament, the Book of Acts chronicles the spread of the early church after Jesus's crucifixion and resurrection. There are multiple mentions of Rome in the book of Acts, including the story of Paul's imprisonment in Rome in Chapter 28. And of course, the Epistle to the Romans is considered to be the most theologically important of all the letters written by Paul, as it is "his most comprehensive and logical presentation of the gospel."[20]

If you are familiar with ancient history, you know that many historians consider the Roman Empire to be one of the greatest, most powerful empires in the history of the world. After 500 years as a republic, the Roman Empire was at the peak of its power from 27 BC to 395 AD.[21] That was right during the time of Jesus's life, death, and resurrection, and includes the time of the early church and the start of the spread of Christianity around the world.

Knowing history helped me and my children understand just what sort of dominant world power Jesus, the disciples, and the apostles and early Christians were up against. The Romans

---

[20] Albert F. Harper, Gen. Ed. *The Wesley Bible* (Nashville: Thomas Nelson Publishers, 1990) p. 1680
[21] https://en.m.wikipedia.org/wiki/Roman_Empire

were famous for their system of government, their architectural achievements, their economy, and their intricate system of roads that stretched throughout the vast Roman Empire. But the Romans were also known for their power, and the brutality with which they conquered their adversaries. Consider that Peter was crucified by the Romans under Emperor Nero, who reigned from 54 AD. to 68 AD. It was the Romans who brutally crushed a Jewish rebellion, slaughtered thousands, and burned and destroyed the Temple at Jerusalem in 70 AD. For 300 years, Christians endured severe persecution and even martyrdom at the hands of the Romans until Constantine became the first Roman Emperor to convert to Christianity and made it the official religion of the Roman Empire.[22] The fact that Christianity spread throughout the civilized world in such a hostile environment of persecution is nothing short of miraculous.

---

[22] Everett Ferguson, *Persecution in the Early Church: Did You Know?* http://www.christianitytoday.com/history/issues/issue-27/persecution-in-early-church-did-you-know.html#storystream

History Resources

If you are yearning to add richness and depth to Bible study for you and your children, look for ways to incorporate the study of world history. A straightforward way to help children visualize when events occurred is to create a timeline. There are many good history timelines and visual aids available for purchase online, but this idea needn't be expensive. I made a simple timeline out of white butcher paper and tacked it to the wall in our homeschool room, and the children record biblical events and historical events as they learn about them. We also have a large world map displayed in our house, and my children enjoy finding the geographical areas mentioned in the Bible to see in which countries those biblical regions are found today.

Good Bible commentaries are also helpful for the task of researching history along with the Bible, as are encyclopedias and the Internet. If you are looking for a world history book geared toward children, a favorite resource in our family is *The Story of the World: History for the Classical*

Child by Susan Wise Bauer. Volume One covers Ancient Times, and it is written in an engaging, narrative style that is excellent for elementary-age students. We also use *The Usborne Encyclopedia of World History with Internet Links* and *The Kingfisher History Encyclopedia.* For the high school student or adult looking to dive into history to an even deeper level, I recommend *The History of the Ancient World: From the Earliest Accounts to the Fall of Rome* by Susan Wise Bauer.

Dig Deeper with Context

Do you think context is important when reading the Bible? For our purposes here, let's define "context" as a full understanding of the time, place, and persons involved in scripture passages. When I teach parenting classes on studying the Bible with children, I like to use the following demonstration to illustrate the importance of context.

Do you recognize the following quotes? If so, can you remember where they are from?

"It's the job that's never started as takes longest to finish."

"Faithless is he that says farewell when the road darkens."

"Courage is found in unlikely places."

"Still round the corner there may wait, a new road or a secret gate."[23]

Those quotes are inspiring and full of wisdom! I can envision those words cross-stitched on a pillow, displayed on a magnet on my refrigerator, or painted on artwork in my house. Some passages might even be worth memorizing!

But though they might sound like wise proverbs, those quotes are not from the Bible. They are from *The Fellowship of the Ring* from J.R.R. Tolkien's *Lord of the Rings* trilogy! Taken alone, each quote is inspiring and thought-provoking in its own right. But the words become even more meaningful when we take them as part of a greater whole and understand *who* said them,

---

[23] https://www.thetolkienist.com

why they were written, and *what* story they came from.

We do the same thing with the Bible, don't we? We pick and choose passages or quotes that are personally meaningful, inspiring, noteworthy, or worth memorizing for future reference, often without considering the context of the story as a whole. There is nothing inherently wrong with that, and I firmly believe God gives us specific passages during certain seasons in our lives to minister to us in our time of need. But the scripture verses become even more meaningful when we understand the period of history and the surrounding circumstances in which they were written. It's also helpful to have working knowledge of the people involved in the stories and preceding events that have occurred.

Who, What, When, Where, and Why?

You may recall from your years in grade school that every good narrative should answer the five W's: Who? What? When? Where? And

Why? We can use the same idea when studying scripture in its proper context with our children.

Who? Who is the author of the book of the Bible or passage that you are studying? To whom is the passage being addressed?

What? What are you reading? Is it a poem? Is it a speech, a prayer or a sermon? Is it a set of laws, or a genealogy record? Is it a story or a parable?

When? When was that book of the Bible authored?

Where? Where does the story or passage take place? What region or country are we reading about? Can you find it on a map?

Why? What was the purpose of the passage of scripture during the time it was written? What is its purpose or meaning for us today?

Most study Bibles include introductions to each book of the Bible that will provide the answers to many of our proposed questions. Bible commentaries are also helpful. The more you and your children know about the context of scripture, the more meaningful the scripture will become to you all. An understanding of context is important for in-depth comprehension of God's Word.

Jesus and the Triumphal Entry

Let's contemplate the story of Jesus entering Jerusalem on Palm Sunday as an example of why context matters when reading scripture.

Now when they drew near Jerusalem, and came to Bethphage, at the Mount of Olives, then Jesus sent two disciples, saying to them, "Go into the village opposite you, and immediately you will find a donkey tied, and a colt with her. Loose them and bring them to Me. And if anyone says anything to you, you shall say, 'The Lord has need of them,' and immediately he will send them." (Matthew 21:1-3)

The disciples did as they were instructed, and brought the colt back to Jesus. They spread their clothes over the back of the colt, and Jesus rode the colt into Jerusalem, where he was greeted by multitudes of enthusiastic followers.

What a strange story! Without context, the assignment to find a donkey with her colt might seem to us like an odd request. However, if you have also read the Old Testament, you know that Jesus riding into Jerusalem on a donkey is a fulfillment of a prophecy and proof that he is the Messiah.

Rejoice greatly, O daughter of Zion! Shout, O daughter of Jerusalem! Behold, your King is coming to you; He is just and having salvation, lowly and riding on a donkey, a colt, the foal of a donkey. (Zechariah 9:9)

If you dig a little deeper into the history surrounding that time period, you will discover that some scholars surmise that riding a donkey was also a symbolic gesture in the ancient biblical world. The horse typically symbolized war and power, but the donkey symbolized peace.[24] Thus, by riding into Jerusalem on a donkey, Jesus was showing himself to be the Prince of Peace.

But there's more! The story of the Triumphal Entry is also reminiscent of another event that happened even further back in the Old

---

[24] https://amazingbibletimeline.com/blog/why-did-christ-ride-a-donkey-on-his-triumphant-entry/

Testament: the story of King Solomon's coronation in 1 Kings 1. When King David was old and near death, his son Adonijah had prepared to usurp the throne. Adonijah was the son of Haggith and the fourth son of David. When another David's wives, Bathsheba, heard of Adonijah's plot, she went to David and reminded him that he had promised that her son, Solomon, would be the next King of Israel. David kept his word, and as a sign that Solomon was the true king, he put Solomon on his own royal mule to show the world that Solomon had his blessing, not Adonijah.

The king also said to them, "Take with you the servants of your lord, and have Solomon my son ride on my own mule, and take him down to Gihon. There let Zadok the priest and Nathan the prophet anoint him king over Israel; and blow the horn and say, 'Long live King Solomon!' Then you shall come up after him, and he shall come and sit on my throne, and he shall be king in my place. For I have appointed him to be ruler over Israel and Judah."
(1 Kings 1:33-35)

With the powerful symbolism of riding into town on David's mule, Solomon demonstrated that he had the blessing of his father as the true king of Israel. Similarly, Jesus showed the multitudes who witnessed the Triumphal Entry that he was their true King as he rode into Jerusalem on a donkey with the blessing of his Father.

By learning with your children and teaching them the *context* of scripture, the Bible will come alive in new and exciting ways. The verses are not just individual words or passages on a page to be plucked out individually; they are a part of a greater whole, a rich tapestry of stories woven together that is greater than the sum of its parts. By teaching the Bible in this way, you will deepen and enrich the understanding of scripture for yourself and for your children.

Questions and Reflections

1. Have you ever studied Bible history or ancient world history? What can you do to improve your own knowledge?

2. How can you help your children gain a better understanding of ancient world history? Perhaps you can craft a fun project like a paper timeline, or visit the library for some books on ancient times.

3. Reflect on a Bible story that you have always found a bit confusing or difficult to understand. Work to study the context and surrounding circumstances, and discuss your new understanding with your children.

CHAPTER SIX

CONCLUSION

And those twelve stones which they took out of the Jordan, Joshua set up in Gilgal. Then he spoke to the children of Israel, saying: "When your children ask their fathers in time to come, saying, 'What are these stones?' then you shall let your children know, saying, 'Israel crossed over this Jordan on dry land'; for the Lord your God dried up the waters of the Jordan before you until you had crossed over, as the Lord your God did to the Red Sea, which He dried up before us until we had crossed over, that all the peoples of the earth may know the hand of the Lord, that it is mighty, that you may fear the Lord your God forever.

JOSHUA 4:20 – 24

I want to finish with some words of encouragement. You *can* create a consistent, healthy habit of reading the Bible together as a family. It may take some time, but you will eventually find that it becomes one of the most special, even sacred, times of your day with your children. Time spent in God's Word together is never wasted, even if you don't feel that your children are immediately grasping every word.

Have Realistic Expectations

Have realistic expectations, especially at first. It may be that you don't get through an entire chapter every day; sometimes, half of a chapter or even less is all that your children's attention allows. That's OK! There will be days when the daily schedule gets too hectic, or bedtime needs to be earlier, or the whole family isn't home at the same time, and you won't get the scripture reading in for that day. Those days definitely happen in my house. And that's OK, too.

Try to reject an "all or nothing" mentality. That's the attitude that makes you think, "Well, I can't do this with my family every single day, so I won't do it at all." Instead of focusing on what you *can't* do, honor God with what you *can* do. I promise you, he will bless your efforts. Take your intentions to the Lord in prayer. Confess those times in which you feel you have fallen short in your example of scripture study to your children, and pray that the Lord will help you be more consistent. God will honor your desire to grow closer to him through reading his Word.

Encourage Individual Study Time

In addition to your family Bible study time, encourage your children to develop their own Bible-reading habits. For older children and teenagers, consider a commitment to separately read the same book of the Bible, and then make a special time during the week to discuss it together. My two teenage daughters love the YouVersion Bible app, and read it on their phones on a daily basis. The updated version allows us to be "friends" on the app, so we can easily see what Bible plan each one of us in the midst of reading.

That feature gives us the ability to select the same devotional plan if we so choose, which opens the door for easy opportunities for discussion throughout the week.

Find Opportunities in Day-to-Day Life

Use everyday occurrences, problems and questions as opportunities to turn to the Word of God. Look in scripture and see what words of wisdom the Bible has to offer about each situation. Here are some examples of everyday crises, with answers from the Bible:

The Crisis: Your son struggles with peer pressure.

This I say, therefore, and testify in the Lord, that you should no longer walk as the rest of the Gentiles walk, in the futility of their mind, having their understanding darkened, being alienated from the life of God, because of the ignorance that is in them, because of the blindness of their heart. (Ephesians 4:17-18)

The Crisis: Your daughter quarrels with a friend.

A friend loves at all times, and a brother is born for adversity. (Proverbs 17:17)

The Crisis: Your teenager struggles with worry or fear.

Therefore do not worry about tomorrow, for tomorrow will worry about its own things. Sufficient for the day is its own trouble. (Matthew 6:34)

A favorite resource in our house for finding answers in God's Word is a book from Focus on the Family entitled *801 Questions Kids Ask About God with Answers from the Bible*. A wonderful reference book for the whole family, it includes answers to questions kids have about topics ranging from Old and New Testament events and people; to current concerns like money troubles, school and peer pressure; to future concerns like death, heaven and angels. Every answer includes a key Bible verse pertaining to the topic being covered, along with a "Note to Parents" section for each question and answer.

Take Your Time

Give it some time. It took us a few years (yes, literally!) to make it through the entire Bible! My goal for my children was mastery; I wanted them to *understand* as much as possible about the Bible, not just hear the words. We went slowly, adding in lots of extra resources such as the aforementioned *International Children's Bible Handbook*, various commentaries, and children's storybooks. The "Read the Bible in a Year" plans are great, but may not be realistic when you're teaching children.

Acknowledge You Don't Have All the Answers

I recently had an interesting discussion with my children about the Book of Job. We had already read through the entire Bible over the past few years, and it was time to start over. My oldest daughter had the idea of reading through the Bible in chronological order, so I found a Bible timeline online that laid out the chapters and books of the Bible in chronological order. Thus, the first chapter we read was not Genesis 1:1; it was John 1:1, *"In the beginning was the Word, and the Word was with God, and the Word was God..."* Then, we skipped back to Genesis.

After we made it through the account of Noah, the timeline told us to jump ahead to Job. For a week and a half, we read together from the Book of Job; but when we got to Chapter 9, there were mentions of Orion and other constellations, and also a reference to Rahab. A lively discussion ensued about when the Book of Job was actually written, and prompted some research to find out more.

As it turns out, Bible scholars disagree about when the Book of Job was actually authored. Some think the story takes place after Noah but before Abraham, because Job made his own sacrifices to the Lord (unlike the Israelites after Moses, who had the Levite priests perform sacrifices). Another hint is that at the end of the

Book of Job, Job shares his inheritance with both his sons and his daughters, a practice not typically performed during the time of Abraham and Moses.

Another theory is that Job lived after Joseph but before Moses, since according to Job 1:8, God tells Satan there is *"none like him on the earth, a blameless and upright man, one who fears God and shuns evil."* If there were literally no other such men alive at the time, Job would've lived in between the lifetimes of the great patriarchs.

Yet another theory posits that Job lived during the lifetime of Moses and was an associate of Moses' father-in-law, Jethro; adherents to this theory also suggest that Moses penned the Book of Job.[25]

As you can imagine, my children had lots of questions for me during this discussion. As you can also imagine, I did not have all of the answers. But the entire conversation made for an animated debate, and inspired even more banter about Bible historians and scholars and their limitations, and how we know what we know about the Bible. We

[25] https://amazingbibletimeline.com/blog/job-bible-timeline/

learned a lot that morning, even though we didn't get concrete answers to all of our questions. The situation could have become a source of contention or frustration, but instead God used it to inspire us to read more, research more, seek his wisdom...and rest in our faith in the One who has all of the answers, even when we do not.

In my quiet time afterwards, I reread some verses from Job 9.

God is wise in heart and mighty in strength. Who has hardened himself against Him and prospered? He removes the mountains, and they do not know when He overturns them in His anger; He shakes the earth out of its place, and its pillars tremble; He commands the sun, and it does not rise; He seals off the stars; He alone spreads out the heavens, and treads on the waves of the sea. He made the Bear, Orion, and the Pleiades, and the chambers of the south; He does great things past finding out, yes, wonders without number. (Job 9:5-10)

I prayed those verses out loud in worship to the Father, and tears flowed as I praised the God of the Universe depicted so beautifully in Job 9. With the same wonder and awe that Job expressed thousands of years ago, I gave thanks and expressed my gratitude to the Lord, that he was so good to draw us closer to him through his Word.

Times of questioning do not have to be scary or threatening. Do not get discouraged! If Bible scholars do not have all of the answers, you will certainly not have all the answers, either – but you can reassure your children that you are willing to aid them in the *search* for answers. There are some questions that we will just have to wait and ask God himself someday when we see him face to face. Your children will come across difficult or unanswerable questions eventually as adults. Train them now to seek wisdom from scripture, but also to take comfort in the Lord's sovereignty when answers are not immediately apparent.

But do not hesitate to seek out assistance if you need it. Over the years, I have taken plenty of theological questions to theology professors, children's pastors, and family members who are in ministry, and everyone whom I have approached has been happy to help us if they can.

Remember Why...

Never forget the ultimate reason to study the Bible with your children: to point them to the gospel of Jesus Christ so that they will intimately know God and follow his will. All of scripture points to Jesus Christ, so let's not miss the point! We do not teach the Bible to our children under the yoke of legalism, or so that our kids will be champion Bible quizzers, or to make them unbeatable in a game of Biblical Trivial Pursuit. We want our children to know Jesus on a deep and personal level, so that he can call them, redeem them and change their lives forever.

In his book *Gospel Centered Teaching*, author Trevin Wax writes, "It's not enough to participate in Bible study as if the purpose of our study is merely to know and love these inspired words. No. The purpose for which God gave us His Word is that we might be fully equipped to do His will. In a very real sense, we have not truly understood God's Word unless we have begun to obey it."[26]

In Conclusion

I began this final chapter with the Bible passage about the monument at Gilgal from Joshua 4. As the Israelites headed into the Promised Land, they faced the seemingly insurmountable task of crossing the Jordan River, which was swollen and flooded at that time (Joshua 3:15). But God had a plan. He instructed Joshua to tell the priests to carry the Ark of the Covenant out in front of the people into the overflowing banks of the rushing river. The moment the feet of the priests who were carrying the Ark touched the edge of the water, God stopped the waters of the Jordan River – just has he had previously done at the Red Sea. The priests stood firm in the middle of the Jordan, and the people of Israel crossed over the riverbed on dry ground (Joshua 3:17).

After all of the people had safely crossed, Joshua instructed one man from each of the twelve

---

[26] Trevin Wax, *Gospel-Centered Teaching: Showing Christ in All the Scriptures* (Nashville: B&H Publishing Group, 2013), p. 96

tribes to go and select a large stone from the midst of the Jordan riverbed. Joshua then set up the stones as an altar at Gilgal, to remind the Israelites of the miracle that God had done. Joshua said, *"When your children ask their fathers in time to come, 'What are these stones?' then you shall let your children know, saying, 'Israel crossed this Jordan on dry land." (Joshua 4:21-22)*

Parents, we can let our Bible study with our children be our Gilgal. Our children will ask, "Why are we doing this? What does this mean? Why is this important?" And we can tell them that we study scripture to remember. Ultimately, the story of the People of God is also our story. We read scripture to remember the unfailing faithfulness, unending love, miraculous mercy and unfathomable grace that the Lord has shown his people from generation to generation. The grand narrative of God's Word compels us to recognize the redeeming power of the Lord Almighty throughout human history, and to remember the gospel of Jesus Christ, who saves each believer from sin and death.

Today my daughter, Sloane, climbed onto my bed and found my Bible still resting on the bedspread from my morning devotions. With some struggle, she picked up the heavy book, set it on her lap, and turned open the pages as if she was going to "read" me a passage. With her sassy little three-year-old's voice, she said with confidence, "*This* is the storybook that changes the world."

"Yes," I told her. "You're absolutely right."

Can we start a revival of Bible reading in our culture? Perhaps. At the very least, you can lead a revival of Bible reading in your own home. Let daily Bible study with your children be a time of gratitude for and remembrance of the miracles and unmerited favor bestowed on your life and your family by our Lord and Savior, Jesus Christ, *"that all the peoples of the earth may know the hand of the Lord, that it is mighty, that you may fear the Lord your God forever." (Joshua 4:24)*

A Prayer for Parents

Dear Heavenly Father,

Thank you for the glorious gift of your Word. Thank you for the ways in which you use the Bible to speak to us, to teach us, and to guide us. We are grateful for your faithfulness, your mercy, your grace, and your unending love for us. We praise you, we worship you, and we glorify you today. You are a Good Father who loves us far too much to leave us as we are.

Lord, we ask your forgiveness for the times that we have neglected to learn your truths because we have not been willing to open your Word and seek your wisdom. God, please forgive us as parents for our unwillingness to teach your ways to our own children; too often, we have abdicated our God-given responsibilities, and given in to the temptation to outsource our children's spiritual education. Lord, by your grace, help us to leave those mistakes in the past. Your mercies are new every morning, and today is a new day.

Father, please help us to make time to study scripture with our children. Make your presence known to us and show us places in our schedule to further invite you in. Assist us in rearranging our priorities so that we might teach our children to have consistent, diligent Bible-reading habits as they grow into adulthood. Teach us how to be the Christian role models that our children deserve.

Lord, you know how deeply we love our children; it's second only to the love you have for them. Thank you for entrusting these precious blessings to us; please show us how to be the best possible stewards that we can be. May you receive all of the glory!

We pray this in Jesus' name.
Amen.

Acknowledgements

I owe a debt of gratitude to many people who generously shared of their time and talents to help this book grow from a dream into a reality. My husband, Skip, lovingly cared for our seven children during many long evenings so I could squeeze time for writing into my already busy schedule of homeschooling, homemaking and childrearing. My precious children encouraged me to see this book project to completion, even though they knew it meant time away from their mother. My oldest daughters, Riley and Reid, diligently cared for their younger siblings, at times late into the night, so I could work with minimal interruption. My father-in-law, Dr. Terry Rowland, checked my writing for theological accuracy and graciously agreed to pen the foreword. My mother, Delana Burch, and mother-in-law, Judy Rowland, read through early drafts and cheered me on with much-needed words of love and encouragement. My editor, Samantha Hanni, tirelessly worked to edit the manuscript, immensely improved this project with her ideas and creativity, and patiently answered the long list of questions put before her by this first-time author. Our family friend and beloved children's pastor, Marcus LeBaron, freely shared his time and resources as we discussed how to improve biblical literacy amongst our children in the church.

I am abundantly blessed with a wealth of godly friends who have covered me with a blanket of prayer during the writing of this book, including Mary, Blaire, Kim, Joanna, Amy and Kat. You are all incredible warriors of the faith, and you inspire me daily with your selfless love for your families as you intentionally point your children to Christ. I do not tell you often enough how deeply I admire and respect you, and how grateful I am that God brought you all into my life.

Finally, I give thanks to my Heavenly Father, Jesus Christ, who loved me enough to redeem me and change my life forever. Everything I have is yours.

"You have turned for me my mourning into dancing; You have put off my sackcloth and clothed me with gladness, to the end that my glory may sing praise to You and not be silent. O Lord my God, I will give thanks to You forever." (Psalm 30:11-12)

APPENDIX A:

RECOMMENDED RESOURCES

This is by no means an exhaustive list; rather, it is simply a list of some of my family's favorite resources. Enjoy!

1. *The Student Bible, New International Version* from Zondervan Publishing House

2. *The Wesley Bible, New King James Version* from Thomas Nelson Publishers

3. *The International Children's Bible Handbook: Answering Questions Kids Ask – Genesis to Revelation* by Lawrence Richards

4. *The Bedtime Bible Story Book* by Jesse Lyman Hurlbut

5. *The Jesus Storybook Bible* by Sally Lloyd-Jones

6. *801 Questions Kids Ask About God with Answers from the Bible* from Focus on the Family

7. *The Story of the World: History for the Classical Child* by Susan Wise Bauer; *Volume One* covers Ancient Times

8. *The History of the Ancient World: From the Earliest Accounts to the Fall of Rome* by Susan Wise Bauer

9. *The Usborne Encyclopedia of World History with Internet Links* from Usborne Publishing Ltd.

10. *The Kingfisher History Encyclopedia* from Kingfisher Books

11. *Family Time* Activity Books by Kirk Weaver from the National Center for Biblical Parenting. See www.famtime.com for more details.

12. *Like Ice Cream: The Scoop on Helping the Next Generation Fall in Love with God's Word* by Keith Ferrin from That You May Know Ministries

13. *Gospel-Centered Teaching: Showing Christ in All the Scripture* by Trevin Wax

14. *Bible Study Methods: Twelve Ways You Can Unlock God's Word* by Rick Warren

15. *30 Days to Understanding the Bible in 15 Minutes a Day!* by Max Anders

APPENDIX B:

SAMPLE ONE-WEEK BIBLE STUDY PLAN

Here is an example of what a one-week Bible plan looks like in our family. By no means should your family's plan look just like ours! We arrived at what works for us through trial and error, and you will find what works for your family in the same way. But my hope is that by including a portion of our plan, you will get some ideas to create your own. While it may look like a lot, our Bible time together usually only takes fifteen to twenty minutes, including discussion time and prayer.

Don't forget to make it FUN! Allow your children to draw, color, paint, sculpt, build scenes with toys, or engage in whatever activity you choose to keep them quietly active while they are listening.

Day One:

- Read "The Story and The Song" (p. 12 – 17) from *The Jesus Storybook Bible (TJSB)*.
- Read selections from the Introduction of *International Children's Bible Handbook (ICBH)*, such as "What You Should Know About the Bible" or "What's in Our Bible?"
- Read questions and answers selected from the "Studying the Bible" section of *801 Questions Kids Ask About God (801 QKA)*.
- Read the introduction to Genesis from your favorite Bible translation.

Day Two:

- Read selections from the *ICBH* section entitled, "In the Beginning."
- Read Genesis 1 along with any helpful commentary or notes your Bible includes.
- Read questions and answers selected from the "Creation" section of *801 QKA*.
- Follow up at bedtime by reading "The Beginning: A Perfect Home" from *TJSB*.

Day Three:

- Read selections from the *ICBH* section entitled, "God Creates Man and Woman." (You will notice that there is some repetition from Day Two; this is intentional! I've found a bit of repetition is good both for review and for reinforcing biblical concepts, especially when the stories get tricky later on.)

- Read Genesis 2 along with any helpful commentary or notes.

- Read more questions and answers selected from the "Creation" section of *801 QKA.*

- Follow up at bedtime by reading "Day 1: The Story of Creation" from the *Bedtime Bible Story Book (BBSB).*

Day Four:

- Read more selections from the "God Creates Man and Woman" section of the *ICBH.*

- Read Genesis 3 along with any helpful commentary or notes.
- Read selected questions and answers from the "From Adam to Moses" section of *801 QKA.*
- Follow up at bedtime by reading "Day 2: Adam and Eve Disobey God" from the *BBSB,* or "The Terrible Lie" from *TJSB.*

Day Five:

- Read selections about Adam and Eve's sin from the "God Creates Man and Woman" section of the *ICBH.*
- Read Genesis 4 along with any helpful commentary or notes.
- Read more selected questions and answers from the "From Adam to Moses" section of *801 QKA.*
- Follow up at bedtime by reading "Day 3: Cain and Abel" from the *BBSB.*

Day Six:

- Read selections about Cain and Abel and the consequences of sin from the "God Creates Man and Woman" section of the *ICBH.*

- Read Genesis 5 along with any helpful commentary or notes.

- Read more selected questions and answers from the "From Adam to Moses" section of *801 QKA.*

- Follow up at bedtime by reading "Day 4: Enoch and Noah" from the *BBSB.*

Day Seven:

- Read selections about Noah from the "God Creates Man and Woman" section of the *ICBH.* The handbook also includes an interesting illustration of the ark and a present-day picture of Mount Ararat.

- Read Genesis 6 along with helpful commentary and notes. Your children might want to read ahead to chapters 7 and 8 to hear the whole story of the flood!

- Read questions and answers about Noah selected from the "From Adam to Moses" section of *801 QKA.*

- Follow up at bedtime by reading "Day 5: Noah's Ark" from the *BBSB,* or "A New Beginning" from *TJSB.*

About the Author

Christa Rowland loves Jesus, loves her family, and loves her church. Christa is passionate about pointing people to Jesus Christ through the study of scripture and through authentic Christian fellowship. She loves to live real life with her family and friends!

In 2001, Christa graduated from Southern Nazarene University in Bethany, Oklahoma, with a degree in Human Relations. She has been homeschooling her children since 2013, and she is the creator of the *Our Homeschool Revolution* website and podcast. Christa loves to connect with other homeschoolers and encourage them on their educational journeys.

Christa and her husband, Skip, are raising their seven beautiful children in the heartland of Oklahoma.

Connect with Christa

Website:

www.ourhomeschoolrevolution.com

Instagram: @ourhomeschoolrevolution

Podcast:

The *Our Homeschool Revolution* Podcast is featured on Christa's website and is available on iTunes.

Made in the USA
Columbia, SC
23 April 2019